Beyond Your Book
Discover the Many Ways
You Can Use Your Book
to Skyrocket Your Success!

by Viki Winterton

Beyond Your Book

Discover the Many Ways You Can
Use Your Book to Skyrocket Your Success!

by Viki Winterton

#1 Best-selling Author and Award-winning Publisher

Beyond Your Book
Discover the Many Ways You Can Use Your Book
to Skyrocket Your Success!
©2013 by Viki Winterton

Expert Insights Publishing
1001 East WT Harris Blvd #247
Charlotte, NC 28213

ISBN: 978-0-9837379-6-4

Author: Viki Winterton
Cover Design: Terry Z
Edited by: Pam Murphy

15 14 13 12 11   1 2 3 4 5

A portion of the profits from this book will be donated to Books For Africa, an organization with the simple mission to collect, sort, ship, and distribute books to students of all ages in Africa. The goal: to end the book famine in Africa.

—Dedication—

"There is no greater agony than bearing
an untold story inside you."
— Maya Angelou

—Table of Contents—

—Introduction—

Books change lives every moment. A book is unique, unlike any other media. Many people try to write a book but only a few succeed. If you have completed your book, you are part of a small, exclusive group of people in this world.

Authoring a book enables you to spread your message and broaden your horizons beyond your wildest dreams.

Your book is the end of one period of work, and the beginning of a more important one. In your book, you can lay the groundwork for your whole life's platform to success. It is not your final word; it can be the start of your conversation.

Your book is your most widely-accepted credential in the largest number of venues. Your book is often your most attractive asset to TV studios, radio shows, speaking events, boardrooms, web pages, newsprint and, most importantly, people's minds.

This book will show you why it is critical to think of your book as a tool that will benefit other people while expanding your platform.

Make your book a realization of your dreams as you think of ways to send your message to your chosen audience. Make your book worthwhile to read, engaging, and with a call to action. Look beyond publishing and selling, to the many creative ways you and the world can prosper from your book.

Your book shouldn't contain all you know. It should be an enticing entry to your world and your current and future assets — your other work and writings, videos, trainings, events, products, speeches, teachings, broadcast, web presence and affiliations — as your world continues to expand over time.

Getting published and having your book out in the market is not the end of the journey. It is the start for you to build your platform, your name and expertise. Tap into this perfect tool to breathe life into your platform and your reputation as THE EXPERT in your field.

"You can make anything by writing."
— C.S. Lewis

—Chapter One—
21 ways to make it big
with your book before you write it!

Beyond Your Book—

Have you ever felt a certain hesitation when you're about to start a new project? You may have had doubts on your ability to fulfill it, or fears of being met by criticism. These are natural feelings, especially when the project you're going to work on is something of huge significance to you.

Writing a book is one such project. You may be able to pour your heart and soul into writing a masterpiece, but there's still the matter of whether you'll earn money from it. Even seasoned authors can't help but ask themselves this question before writing a new book: Will it sell and bring profit?

Thankfully, it takes only a little creativity and resourcefulness to ease your money worries. Even better, you can start making financial headway right at the very beginning – even before you write the book itself!

Here are 21 tips on how to get started on making money from your book, both in your actual day-to-day life and in your online life:

1. Team up with someone who can be of great help. Chances are, there are aspects of book-writing or publishing you'll need help on. Find someone who could provide valuable assistance to you. One good example is getting a reliable publicist who can book you for appearances in relevant events.

2. Promote your book with your current tools. All it needs is a little tweak on your existing promotional tools to highlight your big project. For instance, you can add your book to your business card, saying something like "Author of [insert book title], to be released this year."

3. Promote your book with new tools. You don't have to spend much money to use new promotional tools. With creativity, you can create new materials such as posters and flyers that make an impact. Better yet, try guerilla marketing by promoting in places where it becomes a pleasant surprise.

For example, if you're writing about art, make artwork out of your usual flyers. Or if it's about finances, distribute copies of a useful budgeting checklist with your book info at the end.

4. Be helpful. Take every chance to provide genuinely useful answers to people. It could be something as simple as responding to an inquiry about your industry, or as important as providing a tutorial on a particular process. People will notice your excellent responses, and this will greatly reinforce your position as an expert.

5. Highlight your achievements. Have you received an award in your field? Have you grown a business to double its original size? Are you responsible for someone's success story? Even a long and steady career is in itself an achievement. Mention these relevant milestones wherever appropriate. This will make people trust you more, and consequently, they'll be more likely to support your book, products or services.

6. Build a story around your book. There's nothing like a good story to attract people's interest! Surely, there is an interesting story behind this project. Did your little child innocently inspire it? Is it a product of a rags-to-riches path? Did it all start from a wonderful epiphany you had while doing something ordinary?

Play up this story by practicing several fantastic ways to tell it. Then tell it – during dinner with friends, at gatherings with colleagues, while getting acquainted with a new client. Make it fresh and vivid every time.

7. Immerse yourself in your topic. Deliberately get in the middle of what your book is about. Surround yourself with great people in the industry. See and be seen at the right events. Learn and discuss relevant materials. Not only does this deepen your expertise, it also creates the best environment for your book to succeed.

8. Announce the book and pre-sell it on your website. A professional and updated website is really a prerequisite in promoting anything these days. Create an impactful banner or news announcement that you're working on a book that's to be released soon. Use a sprinkling of strong words like *exciting*,

absolutely, and *powerful*. Add a great graphic or two.

Bonus tip: Learn how to optimize your website to make it appear more prominently in internet searches. There are many SEO (Search Engine Optimization) courses and specialists today that aren't hard on the budget – and the return on investment can be well worth it.

9. Promote your book on social media. Having a business page on Facebook is commonly recommended for companies and individual brands. If you already have a professional profile on social media, then it's definitely a must to announce and promote your upcoming work there.

But don't discount the power of personal sharing, too! Use your personal bio to promote your book using genuine, first-person posts. Also make use of Twitter, where you can tweet varied promotional blurbs everyday. Meanwhile, Pinterest is an amazing tool for referring visitors to your website. Of course, don't forget LinkedIn where you get access to promote to the professional world.

10. Put out book teasers. Take a few points you're planning to include in your book and transform them into teasers that capture attention. This can be in the form of a short video clip, a diagram, or an image with a nice quote, among many others.

The key is to include just enough information to make people feel they're learning something yet also leave them wanting more. And don't forget prominently presenting your upcoming book at the end or bottom of the teaser.

11. Actively participate in conversations. There are countless conversations happening all the time online. There are forums, blog comments, and even discussions on social media. Spend some time participating in the conversations relevant to your book. Don't just post randomly – reply to other posters and call them by name to engage them. Provide your own opinions backed by facts, and you'll get noticed. Just remember to be considerate and sincere. You can even say something like "I'm currently writing a book on this topic."

12. Write articles around your book. Publish these articles in different places, like your own website and article directories. You can even offer these to established newspapers and magazines. This helps create a buzz around you and your book's central topic.

You can write many different articles on a single topic – you just have to look at it from different angles. For example, if your book is going to be about the economy, you can write at least three different articles from the perspectives of a government leader, an economist, and an average citizen.

13. Write guest blog posts. The difference between regular articles and guest blog posts is that guest blog posts are, to some extent, backed by the blog owners. It's powerful proof of your authority. When you write a guest post on a popular blog, you get a share of that popularity just by association. It's even more fulfilling when your post has an author bio or editor's note that reflects wonderfully on your upcoming book. So take time to write a good post targeted for certain blogs, then contribute it. You might even get paid to write more future posts.

14. Prioritize the book in all your online profiles. Remember that your online presence goes way beyond social media. Try to search your name on Google and you'll see that it appears in places you have forgotten or are not expecting. As much as possible, make sure your name appears in a good light and is associated with your book or book topic. Go ahead and edit your profiles, or review your old online posts if necessary. Then wherever you can, mention your upcoming book close to your name.

15. Provide interesting behind-the-scene events. People love it when they realize that behind greatness is a human being who hasn't lost contact with the real world. This is why behind-the-scene events have such an appeal: they reveal the human side of you. Try this technique every once in a while. Post a picture of you hard at work, a clip of something that inspired you that day, or even a simple text status sharing interesting details. One great way to make sure it's interesting to your audience is to ask whether they're likely to experience it, too. *Manic*

Monday and *TGIF* posts, for example, are very relatable. Such posts make people feel that you're a down-to-earth person, and this gains you more trust.

16. Create multimedia promotions. Ever notice how quotes placed on photos spread like wildfire on the internet? Or how YouTube videos can go viral more easily and faster than chain emails? This is the power of multimedia.

People are bombarded with piles and piles of plain text every-day. To capture their attention, you have to let their eyes set on something colorful, moving, or simply beautiful. Promote using some great images and videos taken for or related to your book.

17. Gather related content around your book. As you research for your book's content, you'll stumble upon related blogs, articles, graphics, and the like. As early as NOW, feature them on your website or social media pages, presenting them as good resources to check out in anticipation for your book.

Remember to let the owners know when you're featuring them. They'll appreciate the gesture and might even do the same thing for you. Just stay genuine. Don't go flooding your site with a ton of links in order to get linked back – this practice is definitely frowned upon.

18. Create your email signature around your upcoming book. Include your powerful book title and subtitle. More details in a following chapter on the creation of a title that will attract your target market's interest and attention.

19. Be sure all introductions to you, made by yourself or others, include the news and title of your forthcoming book. This will place and keep the emphasis on you as THE EXPERT.

20. Need to finance your book's publication? There are a number of project fund-raising sites on the web to help you do just that. Here are just a few. Eligibility requirements vary:

www.gofundme.com
www.crowdfundingsite.net
www.kickstarter.com

21. Make it interesting! This is arguably the best tip for anyone writing a book. It is likely to sell if it's truly interesting.
Think about your topic: You know it's good, but is it angled in
a way that will appeal to people? Then think about the
interesting details you can incorporate in the book's contents
and promotion.

Recall personal anecdotes, funny incidents, outstanding experiences, and wonderful life lessons. Most importantly, embody
the interesting aspects of your book! Be the person who makes
others smile, the person who always has something valuable to
impart, or the person who can carry great conversations.

A person like that is hard to miss and will definitely gain lots
of support, whatever book he or she is writing. The trick really
is to find that spark you've gained from your life experiences,
and just let it shine.

As daunting as it may seem, writing a book is first and fore-
most a good project for yourself, and it should be fulfilling no
matter how it's received by the public or how much money it
earns for you. You don't have to be afraid of creating something of value. You do it to leave your mark in the world, and
that in itself is a priceless reward.

But if you could make money out of it, then all the better! With
the 21 ways listed above, even if you use just a few, it's really
not that hard. Think of it as your material bonus as an author:
You're not only leaving a legacy with your writing, you're also
earning for yourself while contributing to others.

Beyond Your Book—

Action Plan Notes:

_____

_____

_____

_____

_____

_____

_____

_____

_____

_____

_____

_____

_____

_____

_____

_____

_____

_____

_____

_____

_____

_____

_____

_____

_____

_____

_____

_____

_____

_____

_____

_____

_____

_____

_____

_____

_____

_____

_____

_____

_____

_____

_____

_____

_____

_____

_____

_____

_____

_____

"An expert is someone who knows some of the worst mistakes that can be made in his subject, and how to avoid them."
— Werner Heisenberg

—Chapter Two—
9 tips to ensure the right topic makes you THE EXPERT to expand your sought-after service offerings and products!

Beyond Your Book—

Are you all set to write your remarkable masterpiece? It is ideal to find your book buyers' profile first, figure out what he or she is eager to learn and read, research to see if it is unique, and then start writing.

Make sure that you have a skeleton guide on the topics that you want to include in your book. This will make it easier for you to compose your thoughts and be coherent with your ideas. Some books that have been published out there successfully gave headaches to readers. The reason behind this — there was no clarity or relationship to the title and its contents!

1. Get Noticed on the Internet and the Shelves

Be very particular in choosing the title that will go perfectly with the topic of your book. This move will make your potential readers take instant notice of your book while scanning through the internet and on book shelves.

A creatively crafted title will entice them to take a second look and grab a copy your book. They will eagerly flip through your book to read the summary at the back.

2. Craft Your Book's Title and Subtitle

Try to be as creative as possible when constructing your book's title and subtitle. Just keep in mind not to sugarcoat your title too much. You will have a difficult time connecting your promises with the contents of your book. Your title should be descriptive, create curiosity, and attract attention.

Three important title tips:

1. Title should be short and relevant to your book's content

2. Title is or contains a keyword often searched for in Google

3. Title is easy to remember

A subtitle will help you position your book in the marketplace, and is necessary when your title needs more description. The title evokes feeling in the reader, and the subtitle is your hook.

Your subtitle should clearly describe the book's title. Use a large, attraction-getting font, and place beneath the book title, or beneath the book cover image.

3. Testimonials on the Back Cover

Before readers will scan through your book, they will flip the book over and read the back cover. What will be included there are testimonials from professionals within your field of business. They need not be famous but if you get the chance to receive some thoughts from experts, it will surely give credibility to your book and to you as the author.

Bestseller marks are not usually included in the first edition since your book still has to gain its popularity and reader base. The importance of a first edition's contents act as one foot in the door of success,. The testimonials are usually not about the business that you are offering. It is all about you and your competence as the book's author.

This is the start of strengthening your credibility as an expert. Once favorable reviews are out, you can start reaping the rewards.

4. Get Interviewed, Quoted and Featured

Your expertise shines when newspapers, magazines, and broadcast feature you and your book. All you have to do is create a press release about your book and send it to the media.

Elements of a good press release include:

- Craft a great hook

- Add an exciting, timely headline

- Avoid complex terms...keep it simple and to one page

- Support with photos, video and links

- Add contact information, and be available for call/interview

(Details on attracting the media are detailed in chapter 4.)

Beyond Your Book—

You can hire a PR firm to help you get in touch with the who's who in the business. Once they do, you may be featured in a specific category. If your book falls under the Trading sector, your featured article may be listed in the Finance section.

Media may run snippets if feature space is not available so it is recommended to include a short description on what your book is about and how readers can benefit from it. One example would be "A Trader for 10 Years turned Millionaire in 6 Months after Using the Most Closely Guarded Trading Secret."

5. Learn to Collaborate with a Renowned Expert

You may start out as an unknown to the majority of your readers, even if you are an expert in your field, but you will become the talk of the town when you collaborate with a big name in the industry. The company you keep can be very powerful.

There are times when a small push is all you need to really go places. You will be respected and looked up to by your readers who want to know more about your expertise.

Collaboration is a tried and tested approach for writers who want to make it big in the *bigger* way. Collaborators are known to be unselfish of their claim to fame and are people who have dedicated part of their success to the more famous who they have always admired.

To be able to reap your rewards, you sometimes have to give credit to your mentors. You are not the pioneer in a field if others have already risen to fame .

Being able to include a well-known author is a good way to start spreading the news that you are an up-and-coming author who has discovered beneficial ways to earn a fortune.

Book anthologies can be a very potent and inspired way to share fame in the pages of a best-selling book and be propelled as an expert.

(More details about the power of book anthologies in Chapter 11.)

Write your book with total authenticity and honesty. There are readers who will ask the same question raised by those who were previously fooled by other authors: "What's in it for me?" You need to answer this the best way you can if you want to be included in the bestseller group. Your information must be honest with the purest intentions to help others.

6. Get invited to functions, spread the word and be introduced

There are numerous events or functions that evolve around the topic of your book. When you join these gatherings, you will be able to spread the word that you are writing a book or have written a book.

If it is possible, bring along some copies of your book and give these out as complimentary gifts. Make sure that you get some information about who will be attending the function so you can personally write a short note of thanks on the very first page of each copy.

This will be your chance to also be introduced to the people who have the ability to spread the word about you. Make it your objective not to hard sell, since people will think you are there to sell and not learn about the topics being presented at the function. Let the spotlight shine on others featured. You will have your time to shine through your own functions in the future.

You can promote your book in a subtle way by preparing business cards to be handed out. Bear in mind that you will only bring along a few copies of your book.

You can also circulate excerpts, a short summary of what your book is all about. You can create enticing copy to enhance your excerpt. Do not forget to create a call to action segment in the footnote of your excerpt. It will usually appear highlighted in a box to give emphasis.

7. Creatively designed leaflet/book excerpt
Use legible font types and font sizes to make it easier for the

reader to read. Do you remember the material that was print-ed in an italicized font style that you threw away after the first sentence? Always remember to design and layout your materi-als in such a way that they are pleasing to the eye.

You may want to seek help from a graphic designer who can assist you with the layout. If you are comfortable and familiar with using different multimedia applications, create the layout yourself to be able to cut down on your expenses.

It is an accepted fact that most writers are indeed creative in nature and they may be familiar with Photoshop and other multimedia applications. This will be a cost-savings advantage for you.

Highlight the benefits the reader will receive in your book.

Choose the greatest benefits and they will serve as the meat in your leaflet. You have to enumerate the important reasons why your book should be read. One thing to keep in mind is to not bore your reader. He/she will not read very small fonts if you have crammed in twenty benefits and included an expla-nation for each of them. Just a simple yet powerful sentence will do for each benefit, or you can think of a phrase that will encapsulate the entire benefit.

Continue showing that you are an expert in your field by high-lighting the benefits the readers can get in your book. An ex-ample is detailed below:

— Gain an in-depth knowledge from an expert trader

— Get to know the well-guarded secrets of millionaires

— A bonus short course on trading at the right time

— FREE ACCESS to the best trading software that normally costs hundreds of dollars

From the given example, your readers will surely be enticed to find out more about your book. You will be bombarded with emails and phone calls asking where people can find your book and your expertise. Now that you have captured their attention, all that is left to do is release the book into the market!

8. URL or link to your website
You do not have to put all the explanations on your leaflet since it will be tiresome to read. Include your website's URL where you can expound on the benefits and other offerings.

Get help in making your website very engaging to increase your online visitor traffic. A .com of your book title is essential, very inexpensive and well worth the small investment. You have to guard your brand, credibility and status.

9. Your contact number(s)
Make it a point to include your contact number(s) in the leaflet that you are going to distribute. This is also a good avenue for the possible publishers, clients, and endorsers to get in touch with you.

Some authors have the chance to be endorsed by a well-known celebrity. If that opportunity comes your way, you may appear as a guest on a radio or TV show to promote your book! There are endless possibilities when you open yourself to the world.

It is important to remember that there are so many ways for you to get the ball rolling before you even lift that finger to start writing your book's first sentence. You will learn how you can start to make money and pave the way for your bestseller even before you search for your future editor, publisher, or marketing manager.

Beyond Your Book—

Action Plan Notes:

_____

_____

_____

_____

_____

_____

_____

_____

_____

_____

_____

_____

_____

_____

_____

_____

_____

_____

_____

_____

_____

_____

_____

_____

_____

_____

_____

_____

_____

_____

_____

_____

_____

_____

_____

_____

_____

_____

_____

_____

_____

_____

_____

_____

_____

_____

_____

"Don't judge a book by its cover"
— American Proverb
(Oh, but we do!)

—Chapter Three—
9 book cover musts to create biz and buzz before your launch!

Beyond Your Book—

Do readers judge a book by its cover? You bet they do!

Your book cover needs to grab the reader's attention, and set expectations for what they will find on the pages inside.

1. **Book Title:**

Put yourself in the reader's place when making your final decision for your book's title. Will your title make sense to the reader? Will it be easy to recall? Does it convey your message and the cover design? Does it supply the reader with the clarity of your intention? Is the web domain available for your title?

Your title should be legible at a glance. Keep your title simple and under 4 words. Use a bold, large readable font. Some recommended type faces to consider are:

Garamond, **Bodoni**, **IMPACT** and **Gill Sans.**

2. **Subtitle:**

Use your book's subtitle to clearly describe the book's title. A good subtitle provides a line of copy which enhances your title, and includes searchable keywords that are not in your title. Use a large, readable font and place it beneath the title or the cover image.

3. **Color:**

Use contrasting tones, and only 2 or 3 colors. Your book will appear in black and white in some publications, so it needs to look good in color and black and white.

4. **Images:**

Choose one strong image that helps people remember your book and is compatible with your title. Place the image in the center or balance it with the title.

5. **Author name:**

Place your name at the bottom of the cover. To draw attention, you can reverse type in a colored box to provide contrast and attract attention. You may also include the title of your other literary successes like "Bestseller Author," or "Award-Winning Author."

6. Spine:
Make it simple and easy to read. Use the same bold, block type as your cover title, and make it readable sideways. Be sure it has contrast to be noticed and easily attract the attention of potential readers in book stores.

7. Back cover:
Place your book title and subtitle on the back cover at the top, a little smaller than on front cover. Beneath that, include a summary of the book, then your bio with the barcode on the bottom to the right.

Potential book buyers view the front cover and then flip to the back cover to confirm their interest. Once again, keep your book summary simple, short and easy to read. This should work like a promotion of your book and give readers a preview for what to expect.

8. Bio:
Share who you are and your recent accomplishments. Stay around two sentences to establish your credibility for non-fiction books and your individuality for fiction books. Knowing about you will help readers to connect with you and your book in a personal and special way.

9. Endorsements and Reviews:
Endorsements and reviews will add to the credibility of your book. If you have quality endorsements from well-known experts in your niche, you may want to replace your bio with the endorsements and place your bio on the inside back of the book.

Two to four endorsements will fit on your book's back cover. You can always place additional endorsements on the inside of the book.

If you have an endorsement from a well-known celebrity, you may want to consider mentioning it on your front cover.

(More about securing endorsements in Chapter 8.)

Beyond Your Book—

The next step is to ensure that your book and cover image are ecognized by the who's who in the field of your topic to elevate your status as THE EXPERT in your niche.

Writing as a passion is a wonderful gift. It draws people to respect you and consider you as an expert in your chosen field, but is it enough?

In order to sell your book and reach the right target market, you need to create a business out of your book. By coming up with a marketing strategy that creates a buzz among targeted readers even before you launch your published book, you can generate tremendous interest and momentum.

Presence on Social Networking Sites
The easiest way to get your message across is by opening accounts and become active on Twitter, Facebook, and LinkedIn. Post daily tweets about quotes that can be related to your book and display your book cover. You can even quote yourself since it is your page. You can also start a book fan page.

To make your time as productive as possible, you can always synchronize your Twitter and Facebook accounts to automatically display a new article, update, or statement that you have posted in your blog. At the time of this writing, free services to schedule your social media posts include: Hootsuite, LaterBro, CoTweet, Twaitter, FutureTweets, Tweetsqueue, Dynamic Tweets, and Taweet.

Those offering pricing plans for service are: Objective Marketer, SocialTALK, Vitrue, AMP, Postling, Sendible, Buzzom Premium, Media Funnel, Converse, and SocialOomph.

Your Colleges, Universities – Visit and Promote
If this is applicable to the topic of your book, it is always helpful to return to your alma mater and request to be included in their newsletter and state there the target date of your book launch. Discuss with the current dean together with the student body president about the possibility of presenting the importance of your book to studies and future employment.

Do Your Homework – Follow the Sites of Bloggers

Make your presence known on popular blog sites. The best way for you to create a buzz that you will be launching a book is to comment and give praises in the comment fields.

By stating your intentions about helping others to participate or invest in your business, you are considered a real human being and not a spamming robot. Always leave your website's URL at the end of your comment where allowed.

One tip is to include on your website, the links to blogs that you visit regularly. This will be a win-win strategy since you benefit from the customer and reader clicks, increase likes, and you will spread the word for your favorite blog's benefit.

Pre-sell Your Book at Organizations, Your Place of Worship, Charities and on Your Website

Prearrange approval to take preorders for your book during regular meetings and gatherings, and donate a portion to your favorite charity or organization. You can also take pre-orders on your website and accept payments through a shopping cart or PayPal.

Press Kit

A press kit is a collection of written or online materials designed to introduce you as an expert, and your book to the media. This kit should include:

- A cover letter introducing you, your book, and the big benefits to their audience
- Your brief bio
- A list of subjects or timely issues you can discuss
- Brochures and other collateral materials
- A list of suggested questions
- A list of additional publications and speaking appearances
- Case studies, endorsements and testimonials
- Lists of clients, accomplishments and projects
- Samples of your work, preview chapter of your book
- Several high res photos

Beyond Your Book—
(More media relations details in Chapter 4.)

Contests on Social Media
Prepare an entertaining but educating contest about different contents in your book. Have participants submit their entries and follow the questions you posted.

A few days prior to your launch, you are to announce the winners plus their opportunity to get a complimentary and signed book from you. It is up to you (if your budget permits) to include a cash prize.

Line up Partners
Contact partners who can share your book launch with their friends, following and mailing lists.

Never forget the people who you have asked for help. They will be instrumental to the success of your book launch. Keep in mind to choose the right group of people to spread the word on your behalf. You can always reward them with a simple token of appreciation.

They will appreciate your sincerity and will be your constant partners in your future endeavors. That is why it is so important to engage in professional and personal relationships with them.

The media are not to be forgotten once you have launched your book. Continue to build strong relationships with them as they have the power to reverse your success.

Create a Video Book Trailer
Design a video, or hire a professional videographer to create a book trailer and promotion for you.

It is easy to create your own with great and easy tools now available on the web. My favorite is <u>animoto.com</u>, which allows you to use video, text, photos and copyright free music to create great results in just minutes.

Once you have the video completed, circulate it on the web to receive great exposure and buzz before your book is published. Top free video sharing sites at the time of this writing include YouTube, Vimeo, Veoh, Metacafe, Facebook, Twitter and Flickr.

Build a Book Splash Page
"What is a splash page?" It is not an invitation for a swimming event but rather, it is part of your website.

The purpose of having a splash page is to acquire the email addresses of those who have visited your website. They will be your potential buyers when you have announced your target launch date.

The splash page is the medium where you can post your target launch date, who will carry your book, and some sneak peeks into the book. Also on this page, you will be able to carry on a conversation and even presell your book before its release.

To be able to build a following, increase your popularity, and claim your credibility, it is a good move to include a tab or link to your blog. (More blog details in Chapter 5.)

Your value proposition is a short statement about the importance of your book. Offer an email sign-up field for your irresistible offer, a preview of your book or advance notice of book release. The signups will connect to your database for future mailings and offerings, to increase your mailing list. Your web master can easily set this up.

Also, set up an auto response so when you receive a signup, a personal response will be sent to your future buyers so they will not forget you, especially on your book launch date.

Once again, investing in your own unique book title domain URL is one of the most important aspects of your book brand. Check to be sure the domain is available before your finalize the title of your book. GoDaddy.com offers domain registration at affordable rates.

Beyond Your Book—
Spread the Word
Word-of-Mouth is one of the cheapest forms of marketing. Request that your book prelaunch and launch be included in any newsletters or email blasts you receive or that you know of in the arena of your book's subject matter.

Live Prebook Launch and Book Presentations
A prebook launch is certainly not required, but can be important because it will be an opportunity to get the right kind and amount of buyers who will line up on the targeted release date. You will be able to spread the word to different groups and build a strong following as well.

Timing is the key in just about anything you do. Keep in mind that when you create a buzz, it may not immediately be picked up. Of course, you have to consider your popularity, credibility, and number of books previously released. If this is the first time you will release a book, news will travel at a slower pace. That is the reality behind a prelaunch feeler.

Since timing is the key as previously mentioned, creating noise too soon might not make it reach the right people. When you create noise too late, people will forget that your book was released at all.

For you to plan your prelaunch, you have to consider these "musts" to create a local buzz in your industry. As early as NOW, decide on a doable budget for the following:

Venue
Do you really have to choose a posh hotel for a prelaunch event? This is not a wise choice at all. The prelaunch event is basically a cocktail dinner where you will serve finger food instead of a sit-down dinner.

The latter is more expensive while the former is just right, and the lack of tables and chairs will compel you and your guests to mingle with each other informally. The best venue is a function room that can hold a specific number of guests.

Guest List and Entertainment
This is not the end of your computation. You also have to consider the number of guests that you are going to invite. These
are the media, bloggers, and some top author friends who may
have written books related to a topic or two in your book.

Going back to the press who will be part of your guest list,
what token of appreciation will you give them? How many
attendees do you have in mind? It is best if you make a checklist on the possible expenses that you will incur.

By the way, entertainment costs are a little steep. You may
want to consider hiring a DJ to take care of your background
music instead of live entertainment.

If your book was written in collaboration with another author
whose name is a standard in the business, you also want to
invite his/her colleagues. If you are wondering who the VIP
guests are, they may be the top-caliber press, celebrities, and
esteemed authors who wrote books that made it to bestseller
lists.

Prepare an invitation that you can mail to the guests. While
you are at it, create an electronic invite that will act as a teaser
and constant reminder which you can also send to your guests.

Raffle-Off a Complimentary Copy of Prelease Book
It will be more personal if you include a complimentary book-
signing segment in your event's program right after a special
raffle draw. Think of a standard statement that you will write
down after you ask the name of the recipient. Focus on the
main topic of your standard signature.

Assuming you are in the trading business and your book is all
about how to become a millionaire in 6 months, write your
note like "Looking forward to seeing your yacht anchored next
to mine. Good Luck!"

A Fish Bowl Filled With Treats for Guests' Business Cards
A fish bowl is often included at a prelaunch since it will be useful to house the guests' business cards. Fill it with treats as a

very effective way to thank them for their card. Do not forget to provide a sign-up sheet as well in case your guests have run out of business cards. In any case, you are assured of their contact details.

It is important that you also have your business card printed, handy and included in the book press kit.

Once you have compiled good reviews that were published in newspapers and magazines, get some copies for yourself.

You can laminate the printed features and display these during all your personal appearances!

Online Book Promotions
In the current market, online events provide a fabulous alternative to promote your book globally to reach a far wider market of readers.

Interactive webinars can be a great way to share a preview of your book content with the world. Free webinars where you share your wisdom and actually have an exchange with participants from around the world builds a close connection and makes your book and its subject matter come to life.

You can then post the video to the free video sights mentioned earlier, including YouTube, to live forever.

You can also use live Google+ Hangouts to easily create live video conversations and Web TV Shows.

Facebook and Twitter provide the venue for live, interactive chat gathering, including Q and A.

Hosts of web radio shows will welcome scheduling a show surrounding the topics in your book. Web TV schedulers are also hungry for great topics and interviewees.

The most successful book launch strategies focus on building rapport by combining the power of live, in-person and online events.

"Building rapport is one of the most fundamental sales techniques. In sales, rapport is used to build relationships with others quickly and to gain their trust and confidence." <u>Wikipedia</u>

There is nothing more important to the success of your book and your platform for success than building rapport and support for your book and your life's work.

Beyond Your Book—
Action Plan Notes:

_____

_____

_____

_____

_____

_____

_____

_____

_____

_____

_____

_____

_____

_____

_____

_____

_____

_____

_____

_____

_____

_____

_____

_____

_____

_____

_____

_____

_____

_____

_____

_____

_____

_____

_____

_____

_____

_____

_____

_____

_____

_____

_____

_____

_____

_____

_____

_____

"Think big! Play big!!!"
— Jill Lublin

—Chapter Four—
7 ways to make you and your book
irresistible to press and media!

Beyond Your Book—

Have you ever attended a prelaunch and the actual book launch with minimal to zero press and media attendance?

That is an author's worst nightmare – zero attention or attendance from the people who matter the most.

It is such a disappointment. It is important to secure the attention of the influencers in the industry since they have the power to enhance the success of your book and your business.

You may reason that bad publicity or good publicity is STILL publicity. In a way, you may be right. However, can you really afford being looked at unfavorably by the media?

It is always through good rapport that a book launch becomes a standing room only (SRO) affair. There may be other ways to get their attention but the most followed "7 Ways to Make You and Your Book Irresistible to Press and Media" will be discussed in detail.

The First Way – Get a Publicist to Handle Your Marketing Campaign

You can always hire a PR expert to handle your marketing/PR campaign. It will cost you a lot but it can be worth every single penny if you don't have the time, the PR knowledge, or the inclination to learn how to create great press.

When you seek their services, you will be given a PR plan. This will detail the strategies for approaching the current visibility for you, your book and your business – perhaps no one knows who you are, much less knows that you have a book to launch. Your publicist will get in touch with media for the opportunity to interview you.

You may be given a few minutes of airtime or a portion of their daily or weekly column. For the press, it usually contains snippets of your press release article. This may be the best that you can realistically expect; otherwise, it will appear too commercial for the press.

The media, on the other hand, will allot a few minutes in their time slots. You will be asked questions about your book, but prior to that, they will introduce you as the author.

You will be asked to submit a short introduction about yourself, achievements, and your level of expertise in your chosen field. It is best to start with your credentials for credibility. The more credible you appear, the more curious people will get.

Is it true that writers are camera-shy and elusive to interviews? It depends on the need. In your case, you have a book to launch and this opportunity is one of the best.

If your publicist is handling your PR or you are going it alone, a good press release is essential to attract media attention.

Press Release Elements
A good press release is a news story, written in third person, that is newsworthy to an editor or reporter.

1. Start with a powerful, timely, hard-hitting headline.

2. The Press Release Subhead presents your angle and hooks interest.

3. The Press Release Lead is the first paragraph providing the facts; who, what, where and when.

4. The Press Release Body backs up claims made in the lead and headline. This section may contain powerful quotes from or about your book.

5. Keep to one page if possible and include your contact name and number.

6. Make yourself available for your interview at the convenience and often short notice of the media.

Beyond Your Book—

Sample Book Press Release:

New Book Solves Old Problems

52 Experts and Thought Leaders from around the world unite to change lives via groundbreaking book, Ready, Aim, Excel!

Charlotte, NC. – January 16, 2013 – "It's about focusing on a future you can change, not on a past you can't change." says, author expert, Marshall Goldsmith. Let go of your fears, try something new, and step into a promising future, allowing these 52 leadership experts and stories to guide you and inspire you along the way. Each conversation contained in these 348 pages is empowering, inspiring, and priceless, and you will find yourself in the pages of these interviews and in these accounts of occupational achievement and personal triumph.

To learn more about *Ready, Aim, Excel!* Please visit
www.ReadyAimExcel.com

Internationally respected authority on business management, Dr. Ken Blanchard, one of the top twenty-five best-selling authors of all time, reveals how praising progress can dramatically enhance your effectiveness as a leader.

Discover the keys to positive, lasting change from Dr. Marshall Goldsmith, Global Leadership Expert and Best-Selling Author of *Mojo*.

Dr. Cathy Greenberg, *New York Times* Best-Selling Author, reveals the most Important Ingredient to success and happiness.

Discover how to quickly and easily turn on confidence from Bert Martinez, international expert on business and marketing.

Expert Insights Publishing publishes books from thought and business experts around the globe. ***Expert Insights Publishing*** specializes in helping people in wide range of topics from money, sales, health and business.

100% of the Amazon profits go to One Laptop Per Child! Bonus gifts await you at www.Ready AimExcel.com!

For More Information Contact:

Name: Viki Winterton
Telephone: 704-966-6647
Email : Publisher@GetExpertInsights.com
###

Second Way: Take Care of Your Business Platform

Prior to your interview, the media will search for your name on the internet. Be sure to always update the blog on your website and other social networking sites that you have joined. An empty landing page will give your publicist the "Sorry but we cannot accommodate your request" response.

Be irresistible to this group by providing all the meat they can chew on. Make your achievements noteworthy, put your accolades in a non-boastful list, and talk about your latest project complete with powerful summary and sneak peeks.

Your background will be checked and if they find even a small negative write-up about you, they may magnify it, most especially if you keep on dodging the question or giving "No Comment" replies.

Keep your online presence on top of your mind. This is the easiest place where the media and others go to get to know more about your personal and professional life. If you want to build your credibility to justify your field of expertise, be aware of your Google image and keep it in mind with every post you make to the web.

The media and press have an innate talent of "sniffing" out the juicy news and other things that can be used to help you in maximizing your business platform.

If there are posts discovered that reflect unfavorably on you and your reputation, there are companies that specialize in cleaning up your online presence. You can find them in Google web search, "clean up online presence."

As with all vendors and service offerings, carefully vet and confirm the credibility of the company you choose to assist you with your reputation clean up.

Third Way: Secure Presence in Traditional Media

You may be all over the internet but enjoy zero presence in newspapers, magazines, and on TV shows.

Beyond Your Book—

Repurposing is taking the content from your book and using it to create a number of different products.

When you are working to build name recognition as an expert in your field or niche, repurposing can be your most valuable tool. It can save you valuable time in expanding your enterprise and empire.

Repurposing is a strategic way of taking your book content to a whole new level and harnessing the power of social media to bring your expanded product offering to your global audience.

Your book is actually a treasure box that is overflowing with content that you can use in many new ways to bring your wisdom to your readers and diversify your income streams.

The beauty in repurposing is that it can also help you boost your exposure as an author and an expert on the topic that you have written about, which, in turn, can give your book leverage and generate more sales.

From turning your book content into bite-sized quotes for Facebook statuses or discussing chapters of your book in more creative avenues such as videos and trendy graphics, to creating comprehensive programs and products, repurposing is a remarkable way to give yourself an enormous edge.

1. Repurpose Your Book in Social Media

Social media is a powerful and dynamic tool that you can efficiently use to share bits and pieces of your published book to draw interest from your audience and, along with it, prospective buyers and income.

Posting short yet interesting quotes and sentences from your book can help give your viewers a glimpse of what your book is about, and on top of that, it leaves them with a sensation of wanting to read more from your book.

Your book can also help to promote your expertise and credibility as an author and an expert, and this can increase your followers and fans and help you build up a strong audience.

The first thing to do is to go through your published book and make a list of the sentences and bits of information that you would want to share. Make sure the short quotes you will be posting are those that can draw your readers closer to your book. Keep in mind, however, that some social media platforms, such as Twitter, have a 140-character limit.

If you find it too daunting to keep your social media networks updated regularly, there are several social media management applications that can help you organize and schedule updates for your accounts. HootSuite is a browser-based platform that allows you to automatically post to five social media networks at once.

However, if you want to take advantage of the flexibility that smartphone devices offer these days, you can go for other social media management platforms such as TweetDeck or Seesmic. Use these applications to schedule the list of posts, status updates, quotes, and tips that you've gathered from your book.

Scheduling at least one post a day or a week is highly recommended, although if you have more content to go around, you can schedule twice-a-day updates to your social networks. You can also link your website or your book at the end of your posts.

However, remember that putting links at the end of every post can put your credibility as a writer at stake because a news stream full of links can only give your audience the impression that you are spamming. The key to advocating your published book without looking like a spammer lies in limiting the number of times that you use links in your posts.

Interaction is also an important factor in building your audience as it ensures the people that they are talking with the real author instead of a machine. Spend some quality time on the websites where your audience usually interacts and try to answer some of their questions and respond to their comments.

Beyond Your Book—
How can you be discovered?

It is important to seed press releases to those in print media as well as secure a slot on a television or radio show pertaining to your field of expertise.

An example would be appearing as a guest in an automobile TV segment if your book is all about motor vehicles.

If your business is about trading to become a millionaire in 6 months, the perfect show would be about money matters in the stock market segment.

Be irresistible enough so TV viewers will not change the channel after they have heard a few lines from you.

Remember that it only takes 30 seconds to catch or lose the viewer's attention; that's why typical TV commercials are rather short.

Be as unique as possible to carry the interest of the viewer and the TV host interviewing you. You need not look like a fashion model but practice in front of a mirror and see if you have a habit of making inappropriate or annoying hand gestures.

Does your voice sound as monotonous as that of an airline pilot announcing details while in flight? Add life to your speaking voice and be able to capture your audience rather than boring them.

Speaking of a strong platform, what the media and press look for in a person is someone who is credible, noteworthy, and witty yet exudes a sense of authority in their field. They want you to be informed, prepared but not rehearsed, upbeat and excited, engaging and lively, interesting and compelling.

Agree to join if they position you as part of a panel of speakers who will talk about their respective fields. This is your chance to be considered as one of the best in your field.

Fourth Way: Go Local or go International

As long as you are comfortable being interviewed by diverse hosts, you should not shy away from a global opportunity. It may be true that opportunity knocks only once; grab it while it's hot.

Before you go on air, it is recommended that you watch a few previous episodes of the program to get the feel of how the interview will proceed.

Find out the type of viewers who regularly tune in to the program. It will give you an idea of how to address the questions that may be directed to you.

Fifth Way: Be Available – No Matter What Day It Is

Ambush interviews may come your way like traffic on the expressway. Take the call and agree to the interview.

Keep in mind that they are the ones who called you so this means that they see you as a potential scoop for their segment. That is a huge plus for you and your book.

Sixth Way: Keep Your Camera Handy for Photo Ops and Newspaper Features

You never know when you can bump into a reporter for the daily newspaper. It is advisable to keep your camera handy at all times or use a smartphone that has a camera.

After the interview or short introduction, make it a point to get a snapshot of the two of you. You can use it in your blog posts.

This will send across a message to your followers that you are in the limelight. However, before uploading it, ask permission from the reporter if you may use the picture you have taken.

Showing respect for the media goes miles in your receiving requests for return visits and future coverage.

Beyond Your Book—

Seventh Way: In an Interview, Highlight the Benefits of Your Book

The sole reason you are being interviewed is to entertain the listening/viewing audience with the focus on your book. Use short sentences and simple words to be able to converse clearly with all of the viewers as they might not belong to your target market. You might spark an interest in them and in no time, you have a new group of followers and book buyers.

In following the 7 ways to be irresistible to the press and media, you will be able to convey the message that you want to your followers and future buyers to watch, hear or read and ultimately share with others.

Your book's success very much relies on the first impression it leaves upon your audience.

Will you still need the media after your book launch? Of course you will!

People tend to forget easily and if you have a good relationship with the press, they will consider endorsing your future books, products and projects.

Some Tips for Dealing with the Media:

- Have a media kit ready, hard copy and online

- Respond to requests quickly

- Prepare your website for busy traffic after the interview

- Perfect your message and delivery

- Listen and get to the point

- Use care with your comments

- Be flexible in scheduling and in your expectations

Beyond Your Book—

Action Plan Notes:

_____

_____

_____

_____

_____

_____

_____

_____

_____

_____

_____

_____

_____

_____

_____

_____

_____

_____

_____

_____

_____

_____

_____

_____

_____

_____

_____

_____

_____

_____

_____

_____

_____

_____

_____

_____

_____

_____

_____

_____

_____

_____

_____

_____

_____

_____

_____

_____

_____

_____

"I don't want to go viral,
I want to set hearts on fire."
— Coco J. Ginger

—Chapter Five—

17 DOs and DON'Ts so your book chapter previews can make you a blog and article-writing superstar!

Beyond Your Book—

Finishing the last chapter of your book is not the end of your writing project. Writing a chapter preview is often necessary for press and media releases, blog posts and book reviews, book packaging and cover design, marketing purposes and additional summary sections of your book as you deem necessary. Also when under formal publication process, chapter previews may be required according to the discretion of the book editor.

Never underestimate the influence of book chapter previews as they are your direct connections to your potential buyers.

They will speak for the book on your behalf. They can be your initial or final chance to convince a prospective reader into buying your masterpiece.

Similarly, terribly written previews can ruin your chance of making any deal, either with a prospective reader or a publishing company.

Substandard and hastily written book chapter previews reflect the quality and level of talent (or lack thereof) of the author. Thus, they reflect the worthiness of the whole book.

Not knowing what and how to write your previews will throw your main ideas and presentations into complete disarray.

Vague ideas will lead to more misunderstanding between you and the reader, which makes writing a book pointless.

PR companies and publicity specialists are specifically commissioned to write book chapter previews to make book launches and marketing plans successful. This is similar to how research publishers hire or outsource works for abstract writing, which will be indexed for content syndication and subscription.

The same process makes bloggers powerful endorsers mainly because on the internet, they are considered the opinion leaders.

In book submissions, book chapter previews are also an author's tools in closing a book deal. They either get you a contract or not.

Most publishing companies only require book chapter previews for screening to avoid wasting time on unworthy reads. Do not let your masterpiece fall under that same category.

Many authors do not even know the use of chapter previews, so they are missing out on the opportunity to maximize their resources in selling their books. Moreover, many bloggers take advantage of this and write previews, reviews, and summaries themselves to attract readers to their blogs.

It is very rare for a reader, even for the most ardent bookworm, to read a book without getting a glimpse of what to expect chapter by chapter.

Today, the internet plays a major role in selling printed and electronically published books. The internet uses book chapter previews as main advertisements through blogs, directories, review sites, downloadable samples, and sneak peeks. Needless to say, it is a must to write only the best and most cohesive book chapter previews.

The DOs

1. Read the whole chapter over again before writing the preview. Whether or not you wrote the whole book yourself, refreshing your mental note on the important ideas and sections to be emphasized is necessary to avoid leaving out any important points that may even be your big selling points.

Unless you have a very concise, point-by-point outline of your chapters, rereading your own work will remain a necessity.

2. Outline each chapter. As you read through it, make a comprehensive outline as your reference. This is a practical and easy way to sort out points and quotes for inclusion in your book chapter preview. It will also give a clear structure of things to prioritize and exclude.

Writing in proper sequence makes your preview more reader-friendly.

3. Always put the main idea of the chapter on top of the preview. In many cases, readers or prospective buyers only spend a few seconds reading previews. What can you expect?

A bookstore or online store displays thousands of other choices, many of them bestsellers and written by already established and acclaimed authors. There is no reason to waste time on unimpressive book chapter previews.

Giving a clear message right away gives you the chance to meet with the reader eye-to-eye. It brings the connection down to a more personal level which makes you believable and relatable as an author in so many ways.

The main idea is the foundation of your preview. You should never veer from the main idea so as not to appear to be deceiving the readers by giving them something that is not really in the book. Nonetheless, the main idea should be laid out without going into the details.

4. Stick with the original tone, style, and delivery of the book. A consistent writing style throughout the book should be consistent in the preview. When the chapters are written using formal, passive narration, it should remain so on all promotional materials, book chapter previews included. Likewise, a conversational tone in the book should also be clearly reflected in the preview.

Sticking with the original tone, style, and delivery is important to remain consistent with your brand. Your brand will contribute greatly to your reputation in the industry. This will also get you a specific fan base. Do not contradict your own writing style.

5. Make your arguments clear. Arguments elicit opinions and formed opinions result in interest. As a writer, all you want is for the public to become interested in your work. The public's

paying attention in your direction means they care, and it is up to you how to fan that interest and let it burn into something much bigger and brighter.

The point of publishing a book is presenting a different side of the story, and along the way, changing the beliefs and mind-sets of some readers. This is what you call influence. When an author starts to have influence on his or her readers, the last foundation for building reputation has just been established.

Not presenting any arguments at all defeats the purpose of positioning yourself as an expert and opinion leader in your field.

Similarly, a story conflict should be emphasized in a book chapter preview as it gives contrast and color to your book.

6. Limit your book chapter preview. The recommended length of a preview is not more than a page or roughly 300 words.

For full length books (books with more than 10 chapters), a minimum of 500 words or 5% of the total word count of the book, whichever is less, should be the limit.

You should avoid boring your readers at all costs. Readers who are only browsing for interesting reads have very short attention spans. They reject nonsense and vague accounts. Be straight to the point and only include important ideas.

Take note that important ideas are not always necessary in book chapter previews because they may spoil the whole content. Some important ideas should remain concealed to give the book a surprise factor, making it memorable at the close of the last chapter.

Use keywords. This is not the time to have reservations. You only have a very limited space to entice readers who have very limited patience. These readers scan for keywords – points that pique their curiosity – and of that you should take full advantage. Search for most popular key words at: www.wordtracker.com, and www.wordstream.com/popular-keywords.

Beyond Your Book—

In choosing keywords, pick words and phrases that effectively represent the contents. In other words, use keywords that are forceful and direct.

For example, instead of using the verb "cry," use the word "weep." In a sense, the former is a specific verb that describes a specific action, but in the imagination, it remains generic. The latter describes not just an action but how an action is done. There is no need to exaggerate things – only to maximize.

8. Use only present tense. You need to lock the readers' attention and that is highly possible by imprisoning them in a time that they relate to the most – now! Instead of saying "The chapter will discuss," say "The chapter discusses..."

Following this rule means you make yourself relevant by every means possible. Staying timely is one sure way.

9. Assess if you have clearly bridged your goal. After writing the book chapter preview, assess the whole write-up if it clearly represents whatever goal you have for writing the book.

Is it to educate, to entertain, to inform, or to warn? If the preview looks like something that is written by a different author, then it means it was not written properly.

10. Compare the book chapter preview with the actual book chapter. Once done, read the chapter and then the preview. This way, you can compare them side-by-side and see if the preview really tells everything necessary to pique the reader's curiosity and make them want to read the whole book.

11. Proofread it. Again, the importance of quality writing cannot be overstated. A simple grammatical lapse can easily disappoint and push a possible buyer away.

The preview reflects the quality of the chapter and the chapter represents the quality of the whole book, which is a direct representation of your caliber as a writer and an expert.

The DON'Ts

1. Do not write the book chapter preview like a summary of the chapter. Some writers mistake book chapter previews as mere transcriptions of important sections or passages of book chapters. However, previews are not rundown lists of points or collections of quotes from inside.

This is a writer's own interpretation of the chapter he or she wrote. At the same time, it should always be remembered that this short article is actually a marketing tool that sells the entire book.

2. Avoid lengthy and complex sentences. Reserve your linguistic and literary verve for the main sections. Do not impress with jargon and highfalutin words that only appeal to a certain segment of the market. This will limit your possible buyers and decrease your chances of penetrating a bigger market segment.

Your enthusiasm for writing the best book chapter preview can take you off course. Limit is the byword. A preview does not need to be a literary masterpiece; there is no need to overthink it. It only needs to be clear, appealing, and effective by whatever means is deemed necessary according to the content of the book.

It should be engaging and not confusing. The trick to writing it is writing on the level of the lowest market segment you want to target.

3. Do not transcribe; describe! Again, this is your own interpretation in the clearest possible way. It should not be a repetition of the chapter itself. Be creative but do not go overboard. Transcribing engaging passages for a preview is only acceptable for novels.

Describe the development of your content (i.e. how it is achieved). If it is a novel, at least give a glimpse of the development of the plot, characters, and conflict. It is also advisable to give a chronological account of these developments.

4. Do not include ideas that are not in the actual book chapter. Be honest. It is too late for additional information and sections (unless you are allowed to make some alterations before final publication).

New entries are no longer admissible in book chapter previews because putting something in a preview that is not in the chapter is fraudulent. Just stick to the original content. If you are really itching to add new and developed ideas, or change already stated ones, save them for a new volume or edition of the book.

5. Do not give too much detail. Be concise and not too detailed. You should leave some room for curiosity and questions to be answered. Remember that you are trying to sell a book and not give it away for free.

The main purpose of writing a book chapter preview is to convince the readers to purchase or download the whole book. Do not make it a stand-alone preview that says it all. Do not preempt your own opportunity to earn.

6. Do not refer to more than one narrative per chapter. Quoting a narrative is acceptable but not recommended for all types of books. However, if the need arises, use only one narrative per book chapter preview.

A narrative gives added flavor to the preview, and many readers will absolutely find it appealing. However, the rule again is not to overdo it.

Some great places, with heavy web traffic to submit your book chapter previews as articles include:

Amazines
Article Announce – YahooGroups
ArticleBase
ArticleBiz
ArticleCity
AssociatedContent
BPubs
Buzzle
DevArticles
EzineArticles
GoArticles
IdeaMarketers
RL Rouse
SearchWarp
SelfGrowth
WebProNews

Beyond Your Book—
Action Plan Notes:

_____

_____

_____

_____

_____

_____

_____

_____

_____

_____

_____

_____

_____

_____

_____

_____

_____

_____

_____

_____

_____

_____

_____

_____

_____

_____

_____

_____

_____

_____

_____

_____

_____

_____

_____

_____

_____

_____

_____

_____

_____

_____

_____

_____

_____

_____

_____

_____

_____

_____

_____

"Dialogue is the place that books
are most alive and forge
the most direct connection
with readers."
— Laini Taylor

—Chapter Six—
101 powerful and unique ways to market your book, expand your fans, following and email list!

Beyond Your Book—

So, you are done writing your book. Everything is settled. Now the only question is how you can publish your book and market it to your target readers. Unless you intend to keep your book for your own private reading enjoyment, you have to advertise your book and have the right marketing strategies.

In this day and age, there are so many authors seeking to make their way to the top of the reading lists. With so many available titles and stories of different genres, how can you make sure that your target readers pick your book over anyone else's?

Well, here are 101 pathways to follow for you and your book to become popular and well established. Read on to discover the formula you can use to get known now.

1. **Post your book on websites** like <u>Goodreads</u>. Creating an account and talking about your book will increase awareness and will let people know what your book is about. Plus, you can also interact with your readers on the website.

2. **Get feedback.** Putting up a testimonial/review page on your website is a good way for people to tell you what they think. Plus, it also increases search results on Google and other search engines. The more people talk about your book, the more it will become popular and searchable.

3. **Create a <u>Facebook</u> FanPage.** Face it. Most everyone has a Facebook account these days. By means of a fanpage, you will be able to post links to your book or anything that promotes it. It will also let your fans interact with you and they can also share your page with others.

4. **Tweet Away!** Creating a Twitter account is so easy. It's also easy to tell the world about your book with this platform too. Being a micro-blogging site, you can talk about your book many times a day and answer your followers' questions, as well.

5. **Sign up for Google Authorship.** Your book will make its way to Google Books. This is one of the most popular

6. **Online book tours are also all the rage these days.** Have any blogger friends? Ask them if they can help out in reviewing your book on their blogs. You can have this snowball by asking their other blogger friends to help out in promoting your book as well.

7. **Clean up your social footprint.** You need a clean reputation for readers to want to buy the books you write as an expert. Whatever you post online stays with you for a lifetime—so be careful.

8. **Ask Fans to post their reviews on Amazon.** It's a simple favor that you can ask from your readers/buyers. Putting up their reviews on Amazon, and hopefully four or five-star review ratings, will help build your credibility and will make people more interested in buying your book.

9. **Hire SEO copywriters.** SEO or Search Engine Optimization is one reliable way for a product to become popular. It helps in making a particular product rise high on the search result pages on platforms like Google, Yahoo and Bing.

10. **Q and A sessions are a must.** You can conduct them via Twitter, Facebook, Goodreads, or even Google +.

11. **Give bloggers advanced reading copies or beta copies**. They can review your book easily and you can then tweak it.

12. **Book trailers** are not only entertaining, but also informative. Who does not visit YouTube these days? Putting up a trailer there and sharing it with the world is great free publicity for your book.

13. **Create your own website or blog with your book's name as the URL.** Sites like Webs.com, Blogspot.com, or even Wordpress offer free sites for you to market yourself online. Create your own website and post everything about your professional work and your book there. Having your own website will make you look more professional and you can update it regularly.

14. **Hashtags are definitely helpful.** See, even Facebook has adapted this strategy now. Creating a hashtag "#" for your book will make it easier for people to search for it.

15. **Tag your blog posts.** Putting labels on your posts will make it easier for people to find your book or product.

Beyond Your Book—

16. **Engage online in social networking sites.** Twitter and Facebook parties are fun and effective. Establish your online reputation by being on these sites and demonstrating your expertise in the topics you write about in your book. Being relevant to your friends and circles will increase your book sales potential.

17. **Create a Facebook Group.** Here, you can talk to your fans like they are your friends. You will get to know them better and find out what interests them. This will give you an idea of how to make your book appealing to them. You can even get ideas for a new book to write from your interactions with people who belong to your Group.

18. **Collaborate with other writers** and promote each other's individual works. Help each other out. It will make a whole lot of a difference in terms of audience reach.

19. **Create a Tumblr page.** Put up quotes or snippets from your book. You will see, people will be interested and will start talking to you.

20. **Monthly newsletters help, too.** Once you have subscribers on your blog, they will surely appreciate news from you every once in a while.

21. **Create a Prelaunch page.** Build up the excitement!

22. **Create an interesting book cover**. Beauty is in the eye of the beholder, but it will be so powerful to put up something beautiful so that people will be interested.

23. **Use compelling words in your book.** Not too flowery, but words that will entice the readers.

24. **Be interesting enough yourself.** If people think that you are quirky, witty, and smart, chances are they will buy your book.

25. **Treat your book like a child** – give it all your love and care so that people will see it, too.

26. **Give away free copies of your book via contests.** Everybody loves contests and freebies. Having these promotions will generate interest.

27. **Create business cards and give them away.** Make sure that your information and info about your book is there.

28. **Review other authors' books.** Helping other writers always helps in building your profile and theirs as well.

29. **Google+ Hangouts are fun.** Fans always appreciate a little quality time with an author. Engage them in relevant and meaningful online conversations.

30. **Record your Google+ Hangouts** and put them up on YouTube. You are bound to gain good mileage when this goes viral.

31. **Undergo social media coaching.** You can learn so much from experts on the subject and apply it to your own book marketing efforts.

32. **Forums can still be effective.** Sure, there are so many social media sites right now, but going the old-school route is still productive. Groups with common interests have their own forums. It should be easy enough for you to find forums with members who fit your readership profile.

33. **Never forget to thank your readers.** They'll be happy and definitely spread the word about you. Word of mouth advertising always works.

34. **Ask friends or fans to help out in creating merchandise for you and your book.** Keychains, pencils, and other promotional merchandise are not that expensive yet are able to give you goodwill points.

35. **Ask fans to make their own book trailers** and tell their friends about it. User-generated content is a great way to promote anything online.

36. **Loyalty is always the key to a good relationship.** Never underestimate your fans or take them for granted. Give them freebies once in a while, like copies of your future books.

37. **Polls** are a good way to get to know what your readers really want and think about. Use the ideas you get from your polls to tailor fit your promotional activities towards a specific readership market.

38. **Answer comments on your blog.** This puts a personal touch to your blog. It is important for your readers to know that you are a legitimate entity. Acknowledging your book's readers on your blog tells them that you are interested in them too.

39. **Ask fans to post their photos** while reading your book. This pipes up curiosity.

40. **Be friendly to your fans.** Even if you read something you do not like, be considerate in the way you react and respond to comments and feedback.

41. **Summaries definitely help.** Make sure that your book synopsis is something that will catch people's attention and make them want to buy the book.

42. **Don't be afraid to ask for help** in creating that book summary.

43. **Online magazines are good platforms** to market your book as well. Create one on websites such as openzine and ezine. You can write advertorial about your book and your brand on these websites.

44. **Sell your book on your website as well.** This will make it easy for your readers to purchase your book. You are likely to lose them if they have to navigate to another site to be able to make a purchase.

45. **Mailing lists always help.** It's a foolproof way of keeping in touch with your fans. Do an email blast to announce the availability of your book.

46. **Sign up for websites** that always hold contests and give away free copies of books for early reviews. Check out Addictedtoebooks, Freeebooks and the like.

47. **Create a Paypal account.** It's easier to process payments this way. Most people who buy ebooks and other products online prefer this payment method as an alternative to credit cards or debit cards.

48. **Setup for a Google AdWords account.** When you have advertisers, it's easier for readers to track your book.

49. **Create and join affiliate programs.** This will help you build a network to promote and sell your book and products.

50. **Write a press release.** Prepare something that online websites can simply pick up and publish as is. This gives publications both online and offline a more convenient alternative to having their own writers write reviews or any other type of articles to promote your book.

51. **Write articles about your book** and send them to newspapers. Differentiated from press releases, these articles can take on a more personal approach. You can focus on specific aspects related to your book.

52. **Try writing for online publications** that let you put your own author's byline.

53. **When someone posts a review of your book online, tweet** the link and share it with your followers.

54. **Be open for interviews** — even by amateurs, student reporters and the like. Exposure is always good.

55. **Partner with complementary sites.** You can collaborate with other bloggers or website owners offering products and services that are compatible with the topics in your book.

56. **Hold on-site book tours.** Have a meet and greet session with your fans. Personal contact with your readers will boost your credibility and reputation as a legitimate writer and authority figure in your specialization.

57. **Themed merchandise is great.** Again, you can sell merchandise that has something to do with your book — such as a notebook or a shirt with your book's title or a tagline or quote from your book.

58. **Spread the word out locally** — never underestimate the power of people around you.

59. **Host a book launch party.** You can do this online or offline. You can even have an online countdown until launch date.

60. **Produce printed copies of your book and donate them** to schools, coffee shops, hospitals, restaurants — you'll make new fans and friends this way.

61. **Sign up for HARO** — an SEO site that will help in promoting your book.

62. **Your pages/social media network accounts should definitely say something interesting** about you as a person as well as your book.

63. **Join groups** on Goodreads.

64. **Be creative.** Be sure that there is something unique about you and your book.

65. **Upload some of your book's content to Wattpad**. So many people, especially youth, are using Wattpad — take advantage of it.

66. **Post it on Smashwords.** It's also a good platform to sell your book and be known.

67. **Determine your book's selling point** — what makes

it different from other books? Write about it and talk about it — and make sure to get the word out.

68. **Post reviews and messages on blogs** that create a lot of traffic.

69. **Speak at events that have something to do with your book.** Say, your book is about the fifties and someone hosting a fifties luncheon has invited you. Take that opportunity to mingle with a captured market. You can also provide printed excerpts of your book.

70. **Guest on local** TV and radio stations.

71. **Enlist your friends' help** in spreading word about your book and you as an author.

72. **Do market research.** Know what appeals to your target market. Use the information that you gather to promote your book.

73. **Do not limit your promotions to a specific group**. You can actually have several target audiences. Work on target audiences with similar preferences. You can approach other target audience groups in ways that would appeal to them more.

74. **Put your book up on Stumbleupon.** This website makes it easy for readers to track your book.

75. **Put yourself on Wikipedia.** Lots of traffic goes through this website. Take advantage of this website's popularity and make your presence felt.

76. **Get on Pinterest.** Make images out of some of your book's pages and quotes from the book — then put it up on Pinterest. It's easy, and if even just one person re-pins it, it can be the beginning of your book going viral.

77. **Place "Pin It" buttons to your websites** so that people will easily be able to re-pin your pins.

78. **If your book is fiction,** then you can use images and put them up on Pinterest to describe the scenes and make them more alive.

79. **You can also put up images from your personal life.** It would be interesting for your readers to see you at work. Putting a face to the name is a good way for you to earn recognition as well.

80. **Host a contest on Pinterest** and other social networks. Stir up excitement with user-generated content. Get people talking about themselves while talking about

your book as well.

81. **Create more websites.** More websites mean a wider audience to promote your book.

82. **Web videos are great, too**. Create some that will say something about your book and interview experts on the subject, as well.

83. **Engage in Book Marketing Services.** People in this area will help you in making sure that your book gets out there.

84. **If your book is a love story,** then make a video featuring a scene, put on a good song or two, upload it to YouTube. You'll see that people will start talking about you.

85. **Go the old-school route in a digital way.** Create posters, banners, and cards about your book to give away.

86. **Ask for reviews.** This way, even those who might not think about writing reviews at first would perhaps be convinced to drop a good word for you.

87. **You can actually filter "bad" reviews on Amazon.** If you think that a certain review will not be good for your book and for your image, then just click on "NO" when the "Was this review helpful to you" cloud appears.

88. **If a review violates Amazon's terms,** then you can ask Amazon to remove it.

89. **Amazon Gift Cards are great gifts to give.** Avid readers always appreciate free books!

90. **Subscribe to the Savvy Book Marketer blog on Kindle** to get ideas on how to promote your book better and track your sales.

91. **Ask people to subscribe** to your RSS feed.

92. **Sell your book in alternative formats** like Kindle, PDF, Epub, and Lit. People will appreciate the fact that the book is available in flexible formats.

93. **Create an Amazon book campaign.** This is one of the most effective online distribution centers to sell your book.

94. **E-mail blasts are still acceptable.** If you have a mailing list, go ahead and use it to promote your book. But, be conscious about the way you blast. Don't do it too frequently or you'll end up annoying your readers.

95. **Be active on Linkedin.** It's the most professional so-

Beyond Your Book—

96. **Create an author URL** with your name or pen name.
97. **Use an Author Central page on Amazon** and not just an ordinary page.
98. **Use your own photo** and post your bio on Author Central.
99. **Get some joint venture partners.** These people will help in promoting your book and be able to give away some items, as well.
100. **Take time to establish your reputation.** Do not force things. Promote, Promote and Promote!
101. **And lastly, before doing any of the above, make sure that your book is well-written and offers great value to your readers.**

Now that you know just some of your options, go ahead, and show the world that book!

Beyond Your Book—

Action Plan Notes:

_____

_____

_____

_____

_____

_____

_____

_____

_____

_____

_____

_____

_____

_____

_____

_____

_____

_____

_____

_____

_____

_____

_____

_____

_____

_____

_____

_____

_____

_____

_____

_____

_____

_____

_____

_____

_____

_____

_____

_____

_____

_____

_____

"Use the skills you have in a new way to create meaningful and brave work."
— Jordan Mercedes

—Chapter Seven—
8 ways to repurpose your book for big profits!

Beyond Your Book—

This will help establish an atmosphere of trust and build a solid relationship with your followers, who are also your potential buyers.

2. Repurpose Your Book in Blogs and Articles

Blogs could be the root of your success in your writing career. These free and simple web tools have helped countless writers build up a strong foundation for their career – whether it's presenting a portfolio or simply publishing ideas for everyone to read. This also makes blogs as efficient tools in repurposing published book content to reach a wider audience.

Although most people unintentionally repurpose their books by writing content based on their blogs, others who have started writing books from scratch can utilize blogging and article submission as an avenue for repurposing their book content.

The main ingredients in building up a successful audience and generating sales through blogging are creating an adaptation of your book and calling your audience to action.

Creating an informative and engaging adaptation of a chapter or a section of your published book can provide readers, who have already bought your book, a fresh perspective and new content to enjoy. For readers who haven't had the chance to read your published book, this gives them a quick peek on what to expect.

If you are writing about how to tips, write an adaptation that gives your readers what they want to know and leave them with a feeling of wanting to know more about your chosen topic.

If you have published a novel, you can try to write a prequel or a short side story about the characters. This will make your old readers watch out for the next installment of your book, and your new readers will be interested to know more about the rest of the story.

End your book blog post adaptation with a Call to Action, which is a solid way of enticing your readers to take some sort of action regarding your blog post. This can range from clicking on a link that will lead to your book listing or your website, providing an email address for a mailing list, or simply commenting on your blog post and sharing their thoughts.

Whatever it may be, calling your readers to action actually helps them form the habit of doing something after reading your blog post. A Call to Action eventually makes it easier for your readers to click on your links and purchase your book and products.

Recommended general blog sites:

Wordpress
Blogger
Tumblr
Posterous
Xanga
Weebly

Once again, here are some article submission sites that draw great traffic:

Amazines
Article Announce – YahooGroups
ArticleBase
ArticleBiz
ArticleCity
AssociatedContent
BPubs
Buzzle
DevArticles
EzineArticles
GoArticles
IdeaMarketers
WebProNews
RL Rouse
SearchWarp
SelfGrowth

Beyond Your Book—

3. Repurpose Your Book in Images and Videos

Infographics are a quirky and fun way to learn complex topics in a nutshell, and the growing popularity of sharing photos in social media websites has also paved the way for the use of infographics to make a statement.

In an arena where photos can be shared with just the click of a button, breaking down your published book and turning a section of it into an infographic can help to boost your book's popularity.

With an infographic, you can choose to highlight the primary points and the essential parts of a section on your book. These could be presented as bullet points with short accompanying sentences and will be put in a layout that will make people want to read it and learn something new in just a few minutes.

Content is not the only thing that works well with infographics – a huge chunk of it lies in the design, layout, and the arrangement of the concepts and the images to make sure that it will look pleasing and interesting to your viewers.

Hire a graphic designer to create your infographics for you, because in the world of visual media, the popularity of your book is directly proportional to the aesthetic quality of your infographic. You can get assistance for as little as $5 on http://fiverr.com

Your infographics should be accompanied by a Call to Action at the end of the image, because this will give your viewers additional resources on what to do and where to find out more about the topic that you have graphically discussed. In the same way as repurposing your content through blog posts, you can call your readers to purchase your book or simply read an article on your website. This will help build your audience and your prospective buyers. However, make sure that your Call to Action does not overpower the content that you have presented on your infographics.

To create your own free infographic, visit: http://infogr.am/.

88

Videos have revolutionized the way people publish content on the Internet. With the rocketing increase in the number of people spending the day surfing on video-sharing websites such as <u>YouTube.com</u> and <u>Vimeo.com</u>, videos have become a great avenue for hosting lectures, do-it-yourself projects, music covers and even blogs. Video-sharing websites also make it easy for writers to embed a video on their blog or share a video link through social media.

Using videos to communicate with your audience and build a bridge of trust with them is the quickest way to establish your integrity as an author and an expert in the topic that you have written about. The availability of a wide range of cost effective video editing tools that can even distribute high-quality videos can make it easy for you to make a video about your book.

Create an outline of the topics that you want to talk about on your video. Before starting to speak in front of the camera, try to put yourself in a confident mindset. Remember that the topic that you will be discussing is based on a book that you have authored and published – this means that you know your topic well.

Use a simple video editing tool to polish your video and smooth out the errors that you've made during the video capture. You can add additional links and effects to the video to provide your readers with more resources. I love using <u>animoto.com</u>.

Aside from repurposing the content of your published books into videos, you can also take your video to a whole new level and talk about additional content and tips that are not found on your book but are still related to the topic of your published book. These videos courses can generate more sales for you than your book alone.

When you post your video, be sure to select the correct category and key words for the viewers' easy search.

4. Repurpose Your Book into an eBook

eBooks are another great tool to use as a give-away, an incentive for your program registration or as a paid download on your website.

This is a perfect way for people to get to know you and a great start to your passive income flow!

There are a number of ways to deliver your eBook to the reader. You can use a PDF download. You can provide a flip book format. You can provide an eBook preview as your irresistible offer for readers to opt in with their email, and then offer the full eBook for paid access.

Be sure to include your bio and website link in the back of your eBook so readers can connect with you.

An economical flip book conversion provider I use is: http://issuu.com

Book to eBook conversion services are offered by a number of service providers including:
wisebearbooks.com
www.myidentifiers.com/bowker_ebook_solutions

5. Repurpose Your Book into Radio, TV and Podcasts

Web radio, TV and Podcasts are free and are easy to produce. Use your book as the subject matter for your programming. Broadcast can be used as a platform for you to expand your ideas, where listeners and viewers get to know you as an expert, where you interview other experts and provide a Q and A exchange with your audience.

Free vehicles for web TV broadcast:
www.google.com/hangouts and www.ustream.tv

Free radio hosting with major global audience:
www.blogtalkradio.com

Excellent podcast tools can be found at:
mashable.com/2007/07/04/podcasting-toolbox

6. Repurpose Your Book into Your High End Coaching Program

Once you have published your book and are looked to as an expert, start offering a coaching program. Often online group programs are developed into sessions from the chapters in the author's book.

Create programs at different prices which reflect levels of access to you as the coach and expert. Your programs may include an online coaching program, a group coaching program, a membership site, an inner circle or mastermind, as well as an exclusive one-on-one coaching program. This is a very powerful way to expand your business and enhance the lives of others.

7. Repurpose Your Book into Your Signature Speech

Turn the material you know so well into an in-demand speech for audiences near and far. The spotlight on stage will enhance your reputation as an expert and once again, increase your revenue stream.

Some great places for appearances are listed below. Include offers for your book as a gift or at a discount.
- Local book signings and on the road book tours
- Networking events
- Fundraisers for charities
- Teleseminars, live events and Keynote speeches

You speech should contain:
1. A topic from your book your audience wants to hear
2. Start with a compelling attention getter
3. Discuss some relevant problems people face
4. Offer a variety of creative solutions and free gift

Go to the event prepared and confident that what you have to share is of value, because it is! (More details in Chapter 9.)

Beyond Your Book—

8. Repurpose Your Book Into a Class and Educational Program

An educational course is the natural extension of your book.

Developing an educational product from your book is one of the most profitable ways to expand your product line and diversify your income streams.

The content from your book can be easily converted to a video learning series, online self-delivered class, webinar course, live event or web broadcast series.

These courses can be successfully valued from $100s to $1,000s of dollars in individual student registration fees.

Plan your course:
1. Determine the type of course you would like to deliver and how.
2. Develop a course strategy plan detailing all the elements.
3. Determine course schedule and content
4. Outline the content and delivery of your initial and concluding sessions
5. Determine bonus learning experiences for students
6. Discover the advanced course offering for your students' next steps.

The setup of your course can be done for you.
www.ExpertInsightsPublishing.com

A great delivery system for your courses:
www.JournalEngine.com
www.udemy.com

Develop an Action Plan to put all the repurposed piec-es in place and into action.

1. Determine your main idea and supporting topics.

2. Plan where you will first post your content and how you will expand the exposure.

3. Use the highlights of your content for a teleclass or webi-nar.

4. Post the audio or video on your website as an irresistible gift to new subscribers or charge to download.

5. Now take all highlights and create an eBook for sale on your site.

6. Use book and eBook content as topics for web radio and TV shows.

7. Make the expanded version your first educational course in many.

8. Use concepts to create a multi-level coaching program.

You don't have to use every portion of this sample Action Plan. Choose what works best for you and your following, create your own steps, and enjoy the creative journey.

Beyond Your Book—
Action Plan Notes:

_____

_____

_____

_____

_____

_____

_____

_____

_____

_____

_____

_____

_____

_____

_____

_____

_____

_____

_____

_____

_____

_____

_____

_____

_____

_____

_____

_____

_____

_____

_____

_____

_____

_____

_____

_____

_____

_____

_____

_____

_____

_____

_____

_____

_____

_____

_____

"A celebrity's body is an
advertiser's canvas."
— Mokokoma Mokhonoana

—Chapter Eight—
3 secrets to attract celebrity endorsements, and book project fund raising!

Beyond Your Book—

After you have finished writing your book, give yourself a pat on the back for a job well done. However, you should know that this is only the beginning of your journey as a successful author. The next step is the more grueling task that may propel you to stardom or bury you in anonymity: marketing.

Yes, publishing a book can be hard work, but getting publicity can be even more complex. More than likely, you'll experience some rejection before you find someone who has the leverage of fame to endorse your work.

In fact, marketing is the longest step you will take on this journey.

Why you need endorsers
The key to kick up your book's publicity will be to get celebrities to endorse it to the public. You may also consider generating corporate sponsorships from businesses whose lines of work are related to your book topic.

Many writers make the mistake of publishing their book and failing to look for endorsements. Successful authors will tell you that this is crucial to the public reception of your book and your work. Following are just some of the reasons why you should get endorsed:

1. Word of mouth. When a celebrity chooses to endorse your book, you can rest assured that it will spread quickly through the grapevine. Any professional marketing expert will tell you that word of mouth is one of the most effective means of selling any product.

2. Getting in the right circles. When you choose an expert in your book's subject to endorse your book, you know that you are reaching out to the right corner of the market.

3. Credibility. Aside from your endorser's fame rubbing off on your book, they also tend to build up your credibility as an author. A celebrity's endorsement is a mark of approval that could soon lend you credence to your own claim to fame.

4. Establishing your career as an author. Consider getting sponsorships as the first hurdle which will make everything easier for you in the future. Whatever successful endorsements you may get on this book, you are assured that you will have a good chance of getting those endorsements again, and more on your next book.

Now that you understand just how crucial these endorsements are for you and your book, it's time to consider what you need to do to succeed in this step.

When you start promoting your book to celebrities, here are the three important secrets of the book trade that you need to remember in order to successfully find your perfect endorser.

- The choice. Part of what will make you successful will be how you choose which celebrities and corporations to approach as potential endorsers. Make sure the endorsement makes sense, and be clear about the return to the endorser.

Before you consider writing to anyone, make a **list of criteria** for your ideal endorser. From gender, age, level of expertise on your book subject, target audience, and other specifics relating to your book and their personalities, and write down your preferences. This step alone will rule out several individuals you may have considered before.

Next, list individuals and corporations you feel fit nicely in your criteria, then those who fall into the important categories you listed but don't quite make it. Allow your creativity to flow while making this list, since it will serve as your future database for sponsors and endorsers.

You might need to write a number of letters and make quite a few calls before you get the positive response you are seeking, so just keep listing those names. Don't get disheartened — you are laying the groundwork for not just the present, but for an exciting future as well.

Now that you have a list of your desired endorsers according to your preferences, it's time to categorize these individuals and businesses according to the odds that they will grant your request for sponsorship.

The same is true for big corporations and corporate executives. Corporate giants may pass you over the first time you ask for sponsorship.

If this is your first book, you may want to aim a little lower on the corporate ladder, or go for smaller business groups — unless your book involves charitable work or a nonprofit donation, which may entice the giants to endorse your work.

After you've made your list, the next step will involve some careful **research.** Find out each person's address and contact details — phone numbers, email addresses, websites, fan sites, and everything else that you will need to reach them. If they have publicists, you should perhaps contact them first.

Aside from contact information, it would help immensely if you did a little background research on each individual so you have an idea of how to approach them.

- The request. Now that you know the people you will be writing to, the next part involves forwarding your request to them. You should now consider how you can best approach your target endorsers.

Sending out a generic letter to all of them might be tempting, but don't do it. Take the most personal route.

While the contents of the letters you write will more or less be the same, it's best if you add a personal touch to each of your letters. That makes it more casual, and will put the recipient at ease with you.

This is where the background research will help you immensely. It will flatter them not only because you chose them as prospective endorsers, but also because you cared enough to get to know them. Plus, it gives out a subtle message that you are serious about publishing your book and that you consider them an important part of your book's success.

When writing your letters, remember these points:

- Be personal but still formal. You might turn off your intended endorser by using a too-personal tone in your letter. You can broach topics about his or her work in your letter if this is related to your book topic. However, avoid delving into your subject's personal life, since this is not part of the official business you hope to have with them.

- Even if you use a casual tone in your letter, make sure it's still respectful. Avoid using slangs and slurs since this might offend your prospective endorsers.

- Ask one or two celebrities (the ones you really like) to write your book's foreword or introduction. That's one way of complimenting them, and it will make a great addition to your book.

- Hint subtly at the benefits they will get when they endorse your book — to be precise, additional publicity. You can mention that you intend to place their pictures along with their book testimonial inside the book, or their names on your book's cover. While it might not be much for A-listers, B and C-list celebrities will certainly jump on the opportunity of free publicity. Smaller businesses will also grab that chance, since they may not be able to afford ads on a national scale.

- End with a courteous note and a Call to Action.

Through this, you are sending a message that you consider his or her sponsorship as important.

Beyond Your Book—

After you've written the letter, prepare the things that will be shipped alongside it. Enclose a draft of your book; but to make things easier for the recipient you should also include a brief synopsis or summary of your book. You don't want to lose an endorsement simply because they didn't have the time and patience to read the entire book!

Also, you could make it even easier for them by writing testimonial templates and sending it along. That way, if they don't have the time to spare to write a personalized testimonial, they can choose a template you can use instead.

Before shipping the package, make sure you place a call to their offices. While it's highly unlikely that a celebrity will talk to you personally on the phone, you can at least notify their staff about your request so they will be expecting it. Failing to do so might bury your package in a bulk of fan mail.

Double check everything before mailing the package (or emailing the files if you chose to do it online). And now you're done with this step!

Well, not quite. You will still have to complete the final step and secret to getting celebrity endorsements for your book, which is...

- **Follow-up**. Many authors fail to get endorsements simply because they stop at the first two steps. When they receive no response from the celebrities or the businesses, they simply assume that the answer is negative and move on to the next person on their list, or give up entirely their endorsement prospects.

People are busy. Many of them don't even check their mail personally; more often than not they have a personal assistant to do the work.

Never assume that you've been declined unless it has been directly stated. There are a lot of things that could go wrong after you've forwarded your request. If you chose to send it via snail mail, it could get lost during shipment. If it was email, it could have been marked as spam. What if the only reason you don't get endorsed is because your target endorser never received your request?

It is vital to follow-up your request by placing a personal call to the celebrity's or business's office. After you've sent your request, wait an average of two weeks for any response. If there's nothing, it's time to place a call inquiring about your letter.

During the call, remember to be courteous and patient. You can't expect a celebrity's staff to have your letter on hand when you call. They have busy schedules, and might not have found the time to squeeze your book in.

If you get rejected by a celebrity, don't be disheartened, and don't be afraid to try again. Remember, patience and persistence are the keys to your success.

Final notes

Acquiring great publicity for your book entails hard work on your part, but you'd be astounded by the results when you successfully get the hard-earned results. Get ready to skyrocket to stardom and watch your book and product sales soar after getting that coveted celebrity endorsement!

Whatever level of fame you might achieve, never lose sight of how you began your journey as a full-fledged author. That's the only way you can hold on to your initial success and move on to even greater achievements in the world of writing.

Beyond Your Book—

Action Plan Notes:

_____

_____

_____

_____

_____

_____

_____

_____

_____

_____

_____

_____

_____

_____

_____

_____

_____

_____

_____

_____

_____

_____

_____

_____

_____

_____

_____

_____

_____

_____

_____

_____

_____

_____

_____

_____

_____

_____

_____

_____

_____

_____

_____

_____

"A good speech should be like
a woman's skirt:
long enough to cover the subject
and short enough to create interest"
— Winston Churchill

—Chapter Nine—
4 ways your book can expand your presence on the stages of the world!

Beyond Your Book—

Books have become a great tool for marketing your business, and one of the best free ways to market your personal brand to your target audience is to take on speaking engagements in your field.

Through your book, you can be a more effective speaker and you expand your reach on the speaking stages of the world. You can use your book to effectively set the stage to:

- Market yourself as an expert
- Share your ideas to the world
- Showcase your skills and show your potential clients what you've got

How Writing a Book Can Improve Your Skills and Presence as a Speaker

It has been proven over time that putting your achievements into writing not only adds to your confidence but it also encourages you to think critically.

Putting your achievements into writing also helps you discover your areas for improvement because you get to study them closely. Since you are already aware of your weaknesses, you can conduct more research and improve on them.

This is a great way to improve on yourself professionally so you can land on more speaking engagements.

As a speaker, you are required to speak eloquently to effectively catch the attention of your audience. When writing an book, it is as if you are speaking to your targeted audience, only they are in your mind.

As you proofread your work, you discover which words are more effective and have more weight. This way, you get to improve your choice of words and become a better speaker.

1. Start with your speaker's One Sheet.
Your One Sheet is a single page summary document that gives a concise overview of you, what you talk about and why they should book you. One Sheets are a great marketing tool in the speaker world. It is filled with information that creates interest in you for speaking engagements!

Your One Sheet consists of:

—Your name

—Your contact information

—Your bio and a short personal summary of what defines you and your topic

—A call-out quotation about your topic, testimonial about prior speaking engagements, or other important information

—List of credentials and accolades

—List of events where you have presented

—Several images of you; ideally one from stage and a headshot

2. Event planners are out there looking for good speakers, and there's no reason you shouldn't be on their roster. So to get you rolling, here are a few important tips to help you get public speaking showcases.

—Be the authority in your area of expertise. Your book will serve as testimony.

—Consider speaking free, especially if you are new to the speaking world, or if the event will give you the exposure you seek.

—Know your audience, their challenges and be prepared to present solid solutions. Once you have defined your target audience, you should have a clear idea of what types of events and organizations you should approach.

—Define and narrow your topic to the needs of that audience. It is also important for you to keep in mind how the topic of your speech aligns with your total business plan, goals and ambitions. Speaking is should be integrated with your business goals, your image and your brand.

Beyond Your Book—

—Be specific in targeting meeting planners. Carefully select conferences, organizations and target audiences who will welcome your topic. Also be sure you are contacting the decision maker for the event. Social media can be a very effective tool for making contact.

Tip: Offer to sell your books to the organization in lieu of a speaking fee. Many organizations and educational institutions have budgets for educational materials but not for speaker fees.

—Add a specific speaking page to your website. Be sure to include:

1. An overview of your industry experience, what you talk about and a cover photo of your book.
2. A list of speaking topics.
3. A sample video of several of your presentations.
4. A list of organizations or events where you have presented.
5. Positive testimonials.

3. Prepare for your engagement.

—Study the masters.

—Get transcripts of great speeches and review the structure.

—Know your material so well that you don't need a script.

—If possible, visit the room where you will be speaking. It may increase your level of comfort.

—Visualize yourself being successful and fabulous.

—You may be nervous, but don't announce it. Keep it to yourself for a more powerful presence.

—Your know your strengths and weaknesses. Accentuate the positive!

—Smile! Smile as your audience arrives and smile as you welcome them.

—So you make a few errors; it can make you more human.

—Keep to the time allowed, no more.

—It is NOT about you: it is about your audience and what you have to share with them. Stay outward focused.

—Fake it till you make it. Even if your confidence is low, pretend it is high. Soon it will be!

—Be yourself. People really want you to succeed.

4. Keep the essentials of good presentation skills in the forefront:

- Make eye contact with your audience.
- Move as you speak and interact with the audience.
- Don't simply repeat what is used on your visual aids.
- Use humor in your introduction and delivery.
- Present in a slow, easy manner.
- Only present what you feel passionate and energetic about.

For you to rise among the competition, you need to provide your audience exceptional value. After your speaking engagements, give out a free copy of your book or make discounts available. This way, you can enhance your credibility and gain more loyal followers.

Always connect with meeting planners after the engagements. Building a good relationship often results in return appearances. Don't forget to request referrals!

Beyond Your Book—
Action Plan Notes:

_____

_____

_____

_____

_____

_____

_____

_____

_____

_____

_____

_____

_____

_____

_____

_____

_____

_____

_____

_____

_____

_____

_____

_____

_____

_____

_____

_____

_____

_____

_____

_____

_____

_____

_____

_____

_____

_____

_____

_____

_____

_____

_____

_____

_____

_____

_____

_____

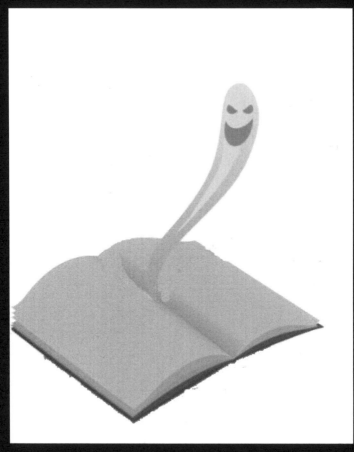

"I turn sentences around.
That's my life.
I write a sentence and then I turn it around.
Then I look at it and turn it around again..."
— Philip Roth, Ghost Writer

—Chapter Ten—
7 top tips for hiring the ideal ghost writer: There is no excuse for not creating a book!

Beyond Your Book—

So you say that you can't write? You can still publish your book. A ghostwriter is a writer who will help you put your ideas onto paper, without being acknowledged for his/her work.

There are many reasons why people hire ghostwriters. Some people want the ghostwriters to promote their business while others hire them to write business letters, blog articles, books and eBooks. Ghostwriters are not only helpful for people who don't know how to write persuasively but they can also provide excellent services to those who have great ideas.

These writers can help you in putting these ideas together in well-written paragraphs, articles, stories and books.

Why hire a ghostwriter?

1. You may have a great idea for a book, but you don't have time to write it.

2.You may want to be known as THE EXPERT in your area of expertise and have your book help you build your platform, but writing is not one of your strong suits.

3. You may have lots of credibility in your area of expertise, but you don't know how to take what you know and turn it into a book, with a unique message to send out into the world.

4. You may already have one very successful book and want to extend this book into a series. If you feel as if you only had one book to write, a ghostwriter may be the answer.

5. You may have your book partially finished and then ran out of things to say. A ghostwriter can supply to rest of the words.

6. You may be on a book deadline and you still have writer's block. A ghostwriter can be hired to make things happen quickly.

If you are in need for this kind of service, the following seven tips will help you find the ghostwriter who can accomplish the task for you.

1. Know What You Want and Need

It's important to determine your wants and needs before starting to look for a ghostwriter. Write down a list of things that you want your future writer to do for you. You need to determine the field of business that you want to promote or the topics that you want to be written by the ghostwriter as well as the kind of writer that you want.

For example, you may need someone to write business letters or advertising articles or perhaps you want someone who can do both. You must also determine if you prefer eBook writers, blog post writers, web content writers, or special report writers.

Also include in your list the deadlines, schedules, and objectives of your task. The deadline must include the specific date and time that you want the task to be completed. You may also add the duration of time for revisions and final editing.

Under the schedules, you need to list the time and days that you want to receive updates about the project. You may also include in the schedules the time that you want to spend brainstorming with your ghostwriter.

In the objectives, you may note the things that you expect from the ghostwriter as well as the reasons why you want to work on that particular subject. Knowing these things will help you narrow down your choices and give you a clearer idea of the type of ghostwriter that you're looking for.

Knowing your specific wants and needs will also help you in communicating with your potential ghostwriter; you will be able to explain more easily your goals for the final outcome.

2. Take Your Time

Don't rush in signing a contract with a ghostwriter. Keep in mind that there are plenty of ghostwriters out there but not all of them can fit the job description that you need. While there are plenty of great ghostwriters in the market, there are also unreliable writers who may just waste your time and money.

117

Beyond Your Book—

Elance, oDesk and Guru are some of the reputable sites that you can browse to find excellent freelance writers. Take time to read the writers' profiles and see if they can meet your demands. Seek writers based on the list of needs and wants that you've written, as suggested in Tip Number One.

Unreliable writers can be easily spotted through their proposals and personal description. You will notice grammatical errors and misspelled words. Their personal profiles may not provide as much information as you need.

On the other hand, excellent writers will only have few errors, if any, because they are aware that proposals and personal profile descriptions are crucial for their potential clients.

These writers will take time to explain their strengths and weaknesses so you may notice their personal description may be longer than those of other writers.

You may also record the names, contact details and profile links of the writers you think are able to provide the service that you need. If you have found many writers, start with those who have already included sample writings and references in their profiles.

Contact the writers who match the job description that you've written. Since ghostwriters may be working on other projects, it would be best to contact them via email first. After you have received a response, you may ask to contact them through other means such as phone or Skype. Take time to talk with your potential ghostwriter regarding the project to know if he or she is compatible to your project.

Listen to the potential ghostwriter's opinions, suggestions and comments about your tasks and determine if you would like to hire him or her.

It would be great if you could meet your potential writer in person. Nowadays, people in the writing field work online, but there are more benefits when you can also work together face-to-face. It is easier to explain your desires and it can make you feel more comfortable in working together.

3. Check Work Samples (Published Works)

Ask for work samples of your potential writer. Many ghost-writers are also published writers so you should also ask for copies of the published works if they are available. Read these writings closely and see if they have the quality that you're looking for.

Other samples that you may want to see are their personal websites, blogs, online public journals and other writings that are posted online. Online posts are recommended because they are easier to review but you need to make sure that he or she is really the one who authored it.

If you completed Tip Number One, you already know what you are looking for. So just read the writing samples or published works that are related to the topics you want the writer to discuss, in case he or she has a large body of work on diverse topics.

In case ghostwriters are just starting off their writing career, they may not have a number of samples to show. In this case, you may ask them to write a brief sample about the content that you need. Usually, short samples are not paid for but you may also consider hiring them for a trial period in order to determine whether or not they can provide quality writing consistently. It will also help you find out if they have the talent that will fit your niche and personality.

If you don't know how to assess someone's work, you could ask someone you know to do it for you. A family member or a friend who loves to read would be the best option if you feel you can trust their opinions.

4. Check References

If the writer says that they have been in the writing business for a while, you may ask him/her to provide references and contacts who could verify the details that you need to know to make your decision. When you're able to get in touch with the references, don't hesitate to ask questions about the writer that you want to hire. It would also be helpful to tell them the specifics that you are looking for and ask them if they believe the writer can do it.

If possible, you may also ask the references to send you a copy or two of the work that the writer has already accomplished for them. Review these writings closely and see if they are the quality of writing you are seeking for your project.

5. Pricing Rate

The rate of the writer will depend on his/her ability to write quality content. It is reasonable for an expert to charge higher rates than writers of less experience.

However, some less than quality writers may also be quoting high rates in order to gain credentials. For this reason, it's better to find multiple writers who could do the task for you. After that, select the lowest bidder.

On the other hand, there are also cases where writers will write based on the price that they're paid for. If the price is low, they may look for other sidelines while working with your project. As a result, you will have no guarantee about the quality of contents that you will get.

Consequently, if the price is right, writers may be motivated to deliver higher quality. There are also rookie writers who are talented and, when they are paid fairly, are motivated to work even harder to provide quality services.

In the end, you have to make sure that you will get the quality of writing that you deserve because it will represent you and make your readers believe that you wrote it yourself. This is why Tips 3 and 4 are important because they will help you determine if the rate is fair.

In line with the pricing rates, you want to also be careful about upfront fees. Some people require this but it is always better to pay in installments as the project progresses or pay in full once the task is completed.

6. Ownership, Guarantee, Warranty and Service Agreement

Don't overlook the importance of signing a contract with your chosen ghostwriter. You need to know that in the field of writing, lots of problems arise due to issues around royalties, ownership, and plagiarism.

You need to discuss everything with the ghostwriter before signing the contract. When you're writing down the objectives and other descriptions about the project, you should also start creating your own set of agreements. List the things that you expect your potential writer to do for you.

It must be made clear that the writings will fall under your name once they have been completed though there may be some adjustments that you want to work in. When the work is finished, there might be some details that you want to add, change or remove. Consider adding variations to your contract in order to prevent future legal problems.

It is important for ghostwriters to protect their rights, so in most cases, you can expect them to provide their own service agreement. Review their terms and see if there are things that you'd like to change. Make sure to record every change that has been made. Keep all the records secured for future reference.

7. Etiquette

Be respectful to your ghostwriter. Show consideration for his or her time. It is not unusual for ghostwriters to have multiple projects at the same time. Unexpected problems will surely arise but always be considerate when asking the ghostwriters about some errors that you detected in his or her work.

Once the writing description and scope of work has been determined, avoid changing it as the project progresses. Don't change deadlines, especially when you're trying to move them sooner. Consultations with other professionals (e.g. doctors, lawyers) are not free so be sure not to ask for additional services from your ghostwriter for free.

Also avoid calling at odd hours. Adhere to the working hours that your writer has established. Try not to send multiple emails. If you have additional inquiries, wait until you've thought about everything you need and send them all at once in a single email.

It could be helpful to ask for the needs of your ghostwriter, too. There may be things that he or she would want to do differently. Knowing specific requirements will help you set boundaries in your relationship. It's important to be warm and friendly to your ghostwriter but always maintain proper working etiquette when it comes to accomplishing your project. When you have a good relationship with your writer, it will be easier to complete the project and it may also pave the way to doing more projects together in the future.

The search for the right ghostwriter may not be easy but it will be worth the effort once you are able to hire the best who meets your requirements.

A good ghostwriter will:

* Help to pull all the important ideas and facts that need to go into your book

* Do additional research

* Help you to organize your facts and ideas

* Put this together with solid and marketable writing

You are the author of your book. The book is your idea. You have the final say on everything in the book.

The ghost writer is the tool you use to make your ideas readable and marketable in a quick, simple and easy way.

Beyond Your Book—
Action Plan Notes:

_____

_____

_____

_____

_____

_____

_____

_____

_____

_____

_____

_____

_____

_____

_____

_____

_____

_____

_____

_____

_____

_____

_____

_____

_____

_____

_____

_____

_____

_____

_____

_____

_____

_____

_____

_____

_____

_____

_____

_____

_____

_____

_____

_____

_____

_____

_____

_____

_____

"I've always been famous,
it's just no one knew it yet."
— Lady Gaga

—Chapter Eleven—
Want to tap into instant celebrity?
You are viewed by the company
you keep in book anthologies.

Beyond Your Book—

One of the easiest and best ways to capture the attention of consumers and make a name for yourself as a writer is to publish or be featured in an anthology. In fact, you may even achieve your goals sooner than you ever expected.

A Brief Discussion on Anthology

An anthology is a compilation of literary works with a common theme. A common misconception about this type of book is that it always features pieces from multiple authors. While this is often the case, it's not absolutely true: there are collections that showcase the works of a single author.

Anthologies are not confined to any form of literature. The most popular collections consist of poems, essays, and short stories, but there are also compilations of interviews, songs, novels, graphic novels, and the like.

Collections are also not limited to a genre. In fact, you can find an anthology to represent each of the major genres, in fiction and non-fiction.

What Makes a Good Anthology?

The compilation should have a theme. A compilation is not an anthology if the works included in the collection do not have something in common. However, there are cases where it is hard for readers to grasp what the theme is; in these instances, the collection becomes seemingly disorganized.

A good anthology is one where the reading public knows exactly what the prevalent theme is because it is evident in each and every one of the literary works in the compilation.

An anthology with works from several big names is preferable. There are a lot of great anthologies in the market right now, but most of these suffer from a lack of star power which results in poor sales and a small following. They may be quality collections, but you can't consider them as "good" because they fail to capture the attention of their target market.

That said, a "good" anthology that will serve its purpose – which in your case is to introduce you to the reading public with a bang – is one that has big names as contributors.

It need not be star-studded – all a good collection needs are a few pieces from one or two big names, and you can be sure that it will make its way to the bestseller list or at least, generate enough buzz for those who are featured and the one who compiled it to be recognized.

The pieces in the collection should be unique. Don't think this ironic just because the first point says that a good anthology is one with an obvious theme. What is meant here is that each of the pieces in a carefully thought-out collection should offer something new to the readers. There may be a common theme that ties all the works together, but each one should at least have something special about it. This can be achieved by including literary pieces from authors with varying writing styles.

Tips When Choosing an Anthology

Now that you are aware of what makes a good anthology, the next thing you should know is how to choose the right one for you. If you choose haphazardly you might end up wasting your resources on a collection that won't do anything for you. On that note, the tips below will help you make the right choice.

Determine your goals. The first thing you should do when choosing an anthology is to establish your goals. If you are a business owner, it may be safe to assume that your main objective for an anthology is to push your company – that is, boost brand awareness for it and consequently, increase your profit.

If, on the other hand, you are a writer, your goals may be different from that of a businessman; your main reason may be to make a name for yourself among the reading public.

Regardless of where you fall, your goals will greatly determine what kind of anthology you should go for. This will be explored

Beyond Your Book—

further in the next point.

Choose an anthology that will help you meet your objectives. To elaborate, if you are a businessman, make sure that the collection of literary works has something to do with the industry you're in. If you're in the child products industry, for instance, you should consider publishing an anthology that celebrates new life or one that explores the relationship between parent and child through essays and short stories.

If you offer IT-related services, a compilation of essays from those who have been part of the industry since its early days may be for you. You can then market it as a "blast from the past" anthology – this will surely pique the interest of your fellow techies and readers.

If you are a writer, on the other hand, you should choose an anthology according to your field. If you are a freelance writer who specializes in philosophy, for example, you should consider a collection of short essays that tackle various philosophical problems. This will showcase not only your writing skills (even if you take advantage of ghostwriting services) but also your expertise in the field.

Zero in on an audience. This is one of the most important pieces of advice given to anyone who wants to write a book. If you are a writer and you don't have a target market in mind, it will be difficult for you to create anything. Or, if you are able to come up with an idea, promoting it will be hard because you don't have an idea of whom you're writing for.

Something similar applies when you are looking into an anthology. If you don't have a group of readers the anthology will appeal to, it will be difficult to market.

Check which types of anthologies are popular today. A lot of aspiring writers "join the bandwagon" in the beginning of their careers – meaning, they write about something that is currently popular with their target audience. Then, once they have already made a name for themselves and amassed a following, that's the time they start letting their creativity flow.

You can do the same with a popular anthology first. If you have no idea what compilations are flying off the shelves at the moment, go to bookstores or visit online book retailers and marketplaces, and then take a look at their bestseller list or browse their anthology offerings.

Once you have a good idea of what topics and genres are popular today, it will be easier for you to choose the right kind of anthology, get published alongside big names and immediately get noticed.

There are three ways you can participate an anthology. You can be interviewed, which requires no writing skills. You can contribute your own writing, or outsource the work to professionals or ghostwriters.

All of these options have pros and cons, but the most important factor is that an anthology is an easy and quick way to get published alongside experts to create enormous impact.

Why an Anthology?

There are many other types of literature, so why go for an anthology? Here are a few reasons why a collection of literary works can be better than, say, releasing a novel.

An anthology is easier. As said in the previous section, an anthology may comprise of pieces from different authors. This means there is no need for you – or the ghostwriter you hire – to write all of the content in the book. It is undeniably easier to create or participate in an anthology than a self-help book or a novel.

It's easier to market. This is especially true if established authors or experts who contribute also agree to market the book. It is certainly easier to promote something with famous names attached to it than a book an unknown writer has authored.

This is because people are more likely to be interested in, and take a risk on, an anthology that includes one or two familiar names rather than one that is composed of pieces written by a single aspiring author who has not published anything yet.

Also, established writers already have a following, so you don't have to exert that much effort in marketing your work – their readers will check out your book even if you don't promote it extensively.

To add to the points just listed, an anthology is also easier to promote because it's likely to appeal to a larger audience. If you've done your research and the anthology has a diverse collection, you can expect more than one group of readers to take an interest in your anthology.

It will cost less. A done-for-you book can be costly, especially if the ghostwriter you hired will be responsible for creating everything and your input will be very minimal. But if you choose an anthology, you can definitely lower your investment.

If you have a special story to tell and experiences to share that will help and inspire others, there is no need to wait to be published **someday**. An anthology can be the vehicle to get your unique contribution out to the world quickly and easily **NOW**.

More anthology details at: www.ReadyAimPublish.com

Beyond Your Book—
Action Plan Notes:

_____

_____

_____

_____

_____

_____

_____

_____

_____

_____

_____

_____

_____

_____

_____

_____

_____

_____

_____

_____

_____

_____

_____

_____

_____

_____

_____

_____

_____

_____

_____

_____

_____

_____

_____

_____

_____

_____

_____

_____

_____

_____

_____

_____

_____

_____

_____

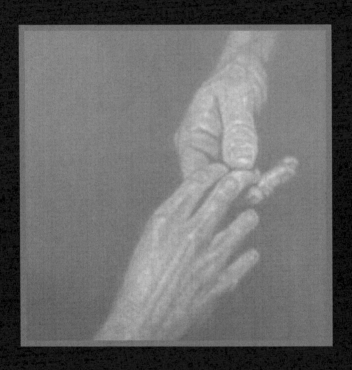

"We make a living by what we get,
but we make a life by what we give."
— Winston Churchill

—Chapter Twelve—
Make a difference across the globe —
contribute to others through your book!

Beyond Your Book—

The insatiable need for individual contribution can be a good explanation as to why we desire to do something to change the world in our own little and big ways. Some of us are able to invoke big and visible changes, while some initiate more intangible changes.

But regardless of how ever large or small the contribution may seem, we may never know the enormous impact we make as authors. What's most important is our desire to change the world.

Our seemingly simple contribution of authoring a book can make a huge difference in our world. It can contribute to individuals and organizations alike through the following ways:

Books can awaken you to many useful facts

Most books, especially text books, are written to present facts. Books can contribute to individuals by presenting different and expanded concepts that they can never hope to discover by just their personal experience.

You may know that you are a living organism or that you are living in an independent sovereign, but you can only know that humans are made of cells and the detailed history of your country if the facts are recorded and presented.

Through books, individuals become more open to discovering new situations and knowing the explanation as to why and how they happen. Through this, the person's drive to discover is not just for the pursuit of knowledge; rather, their desire to discover the truth is also awakened.

Organizations can also benefit from books in a way that they are able to get actual data from those who have already experienced that which they desire to achieve. After all, businesses cannot hope to survive for long if they are not equipped with the knowledge that they need to succeed.

This includes methods on how to create income, reverse losses, and report taxes. Books can also provide them information related to marketing, how to start the business, and other proven systems.

Books can improve thinking and other mental skills

Along with the knowledge that books can provide, reading also improves many of our cognitive skills. And with a better mind, the individual and the people behind an organization can contribute in many ways:

Problems are solved faster

If a person has foresight on what can happen, they are able to conceive solutions before events transpire. Books are a good provider of vicarious learning.

For organizations, being able to resolve the problem faster can also prevent conflicts between employees. Problems encountered in the company (or any group) can cause delays in projects, which can then lead to conflicts and lost income. If problems are solved faster, working relationships and camaraderie are improved, leading to a productive and positive culture within the company.

Ideas are conceived

The world improves when people think creatively "outside the box," and books can be that instrument. As a person reads, their mind starts to conceive ideas that can improve the current living condition. Many organizations have been founded on this very important principle, leading them to build successful businesses.

When a person's imagination is stimulated, creative ideas are born, and what usually follows is thinking about the feasibility of how goals can be realized. This is very useful in bringing innovation to a product and in marketing.

In this way, books are challenging the individual into forming their own ideas on how the world can become a better place through their contribution.

Beyond Your Book—
There is better recall and organization
We are all required to memorize information or tasks. Books can help the individual to develop certain organizational techniques, since most information is written in a well-organized manner. Therefore, the individual is able to improve recall and more tasks to be accomplished.

It can improve concentration
Books compel the reader to sit down, focus, and concentrate on what it has to offer. After all, you cannot hope to gain anything from a book if you don't give your attention to it.

In many ways, books can be used to help people improve these skills, especially for those who lack them.

In an organization, the employee's focus and concentration is one of the traits that employers seek. Even the easiest tasks cannot be accomplished if the employee is not focused on his/her assigned work. This increases productivity, and cascades to the market because of the improved quality output produced.

Books help people to continuously improve
Learning should be continuous; it should never stop throughout our lifetime. Because of the consistent release of editions and publishing of new volumes of a book, the individual continues to improve themselves by improving the theories or concepts that they hold dear.

Similarly, organizations will benefit from the new knowledge when it comes to anything that is related to their line of business. Through books, individuals are able to keep up with the pace of the world.

Books are a source of hope and inspiration
First-hand accounts, self-help books, biographies, anthologies and religious books can serve as sources of hope and inspiration to readers:

First-hand accounts

A first-hand account can be similar to an autobiography, in the sense that it shares with the reader the events of their life. However, first-hand accounts are limited to sharing a specific situation or event as well as how they dealt with it. This type of book can be helpful in removing the reader's hesitation to take the same or similar action.

By knowing how problems were resolved, that the results were successful and that someone also accomplished what they have in mind can give them the assurance that their idea can also be successful.

It can also remove the individual's inhibition, making them think that "If the author can do it, then I can do it too!" In this manner, it can be said that authors are able to contribute to other individuals by "unconsciously" motivating them to pursue what their goals, dreams and desires.

Self-help books

These are considered as a "step-by-step" guide on how to deal with particular situations – mostly, situations that can be detrimental to the individual as well as to others. As the author presents practical tips on how to overcome a specific problem, they are helping more people to become stronger and improve their lives.

This will give readers the idea that they can get over any problem if they learn how to acknowledge their weaknesses first.

On the other hand, most self-help books for organizations are related to dealing with human resource problems like building retention or how to motivate the un-motivated.

These can help preserve the workforce of the company, so they can minimize the losses incurred by hiring new employees, project delays due to resignations, and the strengthening the employer-employee relationship.

Beyond Your Book—

Biographies

These books give the reader a glimpse of a distinguished individual's life. Aside from the success and struggles that they've encountered, it will also give the readers an idea of the featured individual's philosophy on many important factors like career, overcoming hardships, and what they need to have if the reader wants the same success.

Similarly, it boosts the confidence of the reader, making them believe that they can also reach the same (or even greater) heights than what the author has accomplished.

The same goes for organizations. They can focus on the passion of the founders of the company. This is to instill that same drive in the employees and also achieve greater heights.

By intensifying the employee's passion to improve their work for their own benefit and the good of the company, the owners can experience excellent employee performance. People who are dedicated in doing something will usually give their best.

Anthology Books

An anthology is a collection of literary works chosen by the compiler. It may be a collection of poems, short stories, interviews or excerpts by different authors providing varied views.

(More details on anthologies in Chapter 11.)

Religious books

The Bible and other religious books are not only about the story of prophets or the Creator; it can also serve as a way to empower people to be their best.

Through the principles stated in these books, one can draw forth strength to overcome the struggles that they will encounter. It can also be used as a guiding principle of companies, as these books contains moral lessons about being in the service of others.

Books are a means of communication

Aside from the author's way of communicating with the reader, a book can also promote the communication skills of the reader.

Ideas are bound to be shared; in this context, readers are able to contribute more in conversations and discussions. They can also meet new people who have the same or different ideas as they do, which can also serve as a way to widen the reader's views on a particular topic.

A book can also serve as a way to improve an individual's vocabulary and grammar skills. The development of an individual's language is related to being economically independent.

By being proficient in multiple languages, the individual can open more opportunities for employment in multi-national companies and be able to meet and connect to more people around the world.

It can also be a way to inspire another person who has the love for writing. Thus, the cycle of communication is never ending.

Books can help a person's lifestyle

Books can also contribute in a person's health and lifestyle:

Books can reduce stress

Not all books contain serious and direct content. After all, some materials like comic books, novels, and fiction books are written for entertainment.

They can serve as a powerful (and sometimes free) way to relieve stress. Books have the ability to make the reader engage in its content, and before the reader knows it, they have already forgotten whatever it is that stressed them out during the day.

Books in a work environment can also help to lighten the atmosphere, and serve as a way to learn about other possible problems and solutions that can be encountered in the office.

Books can connect, amuse and educate people, all at the same time.

Books can help avert the adaptation of bad habits

Some people respond to stress and idleness by adapting habits that can cause harmful effects to one's health. Two of the most common habits are smoking and drinking. People who want to take their minds away from the stress of work or family will often adapt these habits.

Without books and the interesting content, more people may adapt the same response just to get rid of their stress. And although this is primarily a problem of an individual, health issues can also take a toll on a company when it involves their employees.

Use your book to get involved and contribute

1. Donate a portion of your book sales to charities, and note this in the first pages of your book.

2. Create or participate in book drives.

3. Engage in book readings to the young and the elderly.

4. Donate your book to fund raising for charities.

5. Donate your book to libraries or humanitarian agencies.

6. Make your eBook available for charity fund raising.

7. Speak to literacy organizations to encourage others to read and to write.

8. Gain attention from media and the press for these acts of kindness and contribution.

Conclusion

Books should never be treated as items that are only used to look for the information that you need. Simple as they may be, the book itself can contribute to an individual or a larger group in many different ways, either directly or indirectly.

As authors continue to contribute their ideas and write books, they are also able to invoke changes to the world by invoking changes in the individual.

A book's influence on a person's knowledge and thinking ability, as a source of inspiration, a means of communication, and how it can start the changes in a person's lifestyle are awesome, and should never be taken for granted.

And, its influence on these global concepts all started in a single person's desire and effort to change the world, and write a book.

— Don't Stop Now! —

Discover unique step-by-step formulas for the many ways you can use your book to skyrocket your success!

www.BeyondYourBookAcademy.com

Beyond Your Book—

Action Plan Notes:

_____

_____

_____

_____

_____

_____

_____

_____

_____

_____

_____

_____

_____

_____

_____

_____

_____

_____

_____

_____

_____

_____

_____

_____

_____

_____

_____

_____

_____

_____

_____

_____

_____

_____

_____

_____

_____

_____

_____

_____

_____

_____

_____

_____

"What you do with your resources in
this life is your autobiography."
— Randy Alcorn

RESOURCES

Beyond Your Book—

Made in the USA
San Bernardino, CA
22 September 2013